Intersecting Realities

INTERSECTING REALITIES

Race, Identity, and Culture
in the Spiritual-Moral Life
of Young Asian Americans

EDITED BY
Hak Joon Lee

FOREWORD BY
Ken Fong

CASCADE *Books* • Eugene, Oregon

INTERSECTING REALITIES
Race, Identity, and Culture in the Spiritual-Moral Life of Young Asian Americans

Cascade Books
An Imprint of Wipf and Stock Publishers
199 W. 8th Ave., Suite 3
Eugene, OR 97401

www.wipfandstock.com

PAPERBACK ISBN: 978-1-5326-1623-5
HARDCOVER ISBN: 978-1-5326-1625-9
EBOOK ISBN: 978-1-5326-1624-2

Cataloguing-in-Publication data:

Names: Lee, Hak Joon, editor.

Title: Intersecting realities : race, identity, and culture in the spiritual-moral life of young Asian Americans. / Edited by Hak Joon Lee.

Description: Eugene, OR: Cascade Books, 2018 | Includes bibliographical references.

Identifiers: ISBN 978-1-5326-1623-5 (paperback) | ISBN 978-1-5326-1625-9 (hardcover) | ISBN 978-1-5326-1624-2 (ebook)

Subjects: LCSH: Asian Americans—Religious life. | Asian American theology. | Marginality, Social—Religious aspects—Christianity.

Classification: BR563.A82 I100 2018 (paperback) | CALL NUMBER (ebook)

Manufactured in the U.S.A.   11/13/18

To all kingdom workers of Asian American churches whose commitment to and love of God are making a difference in our society

CONTENTS

CONTRIBUTORS

Daniel D. Lee

Daniel D. Lee serves as the Assistant Provost for the Center for Asian American Theology and Ministry and Assistant Professor of Theology and Asian American Ministry at Fuller Theological Seminary. Serving in various leadership roles since 2010, he has been the key force behind the establishment of the Center and Fuller's Asian American program. His research areas focus on the Reformed tradition and contextual theologies, and he brings broad ministry experience to his work. He is the author of the book *Double Particularity: Karl Barth, Contextuality, and Asian American Theology* (Fortress, 2017), as well as several articles and book chapters.

Hak Joon Lee

Hak Joon Lee is Lewis B. Smedes Professor of Christian Ethics at Fuller Theological Seminary. Lee has published several books, including *The Great World House: Martin Luther King, Jr. and Global Ethics* (Pilgrim, 2011), as well as numerous articles. He is currently working on two manuscripts under contract: *An Invitation to Christian Social Ethics: Diverse Responses to Divisive Issues* (coedited with Tim Dearborn, IVP Academic), and *New Covenant Ethics: Methodology and Practice* (Eerdmans). Additionally, in 2007, Lee founded G2G Christian Education Center, a research institute on Asian American Christianity and culture. Through the Center, he has published several contextually grounded curricula for Korean North American youth (in English) and their parents (in Korean).

Jeff M. Liou

Jeff M. Liou is the Protestant Chaplain for the seven Claremont Colleges and Commissioned Pastor in the Christian Reformed Church of North America. His ministry to college students and young adults began in 2001, leading him to a wide variety of campus, church, and parachurch ministries. He earned his PhD in Theology and Culture with a focus on race and ethnicity from Fuller Theological Seminary, where he is Adjunct Assistant Professor of Ethics. Dr. Liou is married to Lisa, and they have two biracial children, ages twelve and nine. On the weekends, Dr. Liou can be found in the garage, restoring antique hand tools and learning traditional woodworking.

Kirsten Sonkyo Oh

An ordained elder in the United Methodist Church, Kirsten S. Oh is Professor of Practical Theology at Azusa Pacific University and the Ecclesiastical Associate Professor of United Methodist Studies at Fuller Theological Seminary. She holds a PhD in Theology with Pastoral Care and Counseling Emphasis and focuses her research on Intercultural Narrative Counseling, Intersections of Identity, and Pastoral Theology, utilizing multidisciplinary approaches. With the priority to live life to the fullest, Oh enjoys various types of music, swimming, hiking, and traveling with her husband, Scott, and daughter, Daniella.

Janette H. Ok

Janette H. Ok is Assistant Professor of Biblical Studies at Azusa Pacific Seminary, Azusa Pacific University. She conducts research on 1 Peter and the formation of early Christian identity and is interested in Asian American, intersectional, feminist, and social-scientific approaches to biblical interpretation. Ok earned her PhD from Princeton Theological Seminary in Biblical Studies: New Testament. She is an interdisciplinary scholar with a practical focus on church ministry and leadership, and serves as a pastor at Ekko Church in Anaheim, California.

FOREWORD

Ken Fong

The way some folks tell it, I was one of the earliest people to start wondering aloud whether being "Asian," "American," and "Christian" were components of a budding and distinctive demographic amalgam that needed to be researched, grasped, and then broadcast, as I anticipated the coming explosion of Asian American ministries. However, back in the eighties when I began searching for valid sources on subjects related to Asian American Christians to bolster my dissertation, I soon discovered that no one was writing about whether being shame-based (not guilt-based) affected how people like me understand and embody the gospel of Christ. I didn't find any material that underscored the need to tailor approaches to discipleship, worship, or preaching to Asian Americans. It was truly a desert.

I did what I could with the scant resources I found on Asian American assimilation and acculturation, extrapolating and experimenting in my context of serving at a historically Japanese American church in the Los Angeles basin, which was becoming more pan-Asian American and multiethnic. By the grace of God and because I'm not afraid of making mistakes, we learned some things that have borne lasting fruit in the ensuing decades till today. However, our learning was limited and isolated. Growing numbers of Asian American ministries were still left to their own devices, some vaguely aware of substantial misalignments with the prevailing European American Western Christian memes and paradigms, but not sure how to calibrate their approaches to fit their people.

Since I began my own exploration of this topic, there have been a smattering of books, some authored by friends and colleagues, that have helped bring attention to this prevailing need. When I began as the affiliate adjunct professor of Asian American church studies at Fuller Theological Seminary in 2015, it became even more apparent that the few existing books I could find either did not cover enough ground or didn't do so in an academically robust way.

So you can understand my heartfelt exhilaration about the book you're holding. To my knowledge, this is the most comprehensive, deep-diving book on the subject of improving the spiritual and moral lives of Asian American Christian young adults. Edited by my good friend and colleague Dr. Hak Joon Lee, the five contributors are each highly qualified to tackle their topics in ways that are both academically sound and experientially tested. Their ten chapters address essential areas that are often ignored or glossed over in Asian American ministries. Yet these areas are where the vast majority of Asian American Christians live and struggle.

I've been waiting for over thirty years for a book like this to be written. This should be required reading for every Asian American Christian and for every person who feels called to minister to Asian Americans. The wait is finally over.

PREFACE

A sian Americans are the fastest growing racial group in the US. According to the 2010 Census, the estimated number of US residents of Asian descent is over 17 million, and growing rapidly; the percentage growth of the Asian population between 2000 and 2010 is an astounding 46 percent, easily topping the growth of any other major racial group. Interestingly, a Gallup poll in 2010 reports that Christianity is the most preferred religion (42 percent) among Asian Americans.

Reflecting this demographic shift and their cultural traditions, Asian Americans enter colleges at a higher rate than any other racial group in the United States. Many of these students identify themselves as evangelical Christians, and their participation in leadership roles at evangelical campus ministry groups have significantly increased. These campus ministry groups serve an important spiritual and social function for them. As college life can be and often is a culture shock to Asian American Christian students—due to the ubiquity of casual sex, liberal use of alcohol and drugs, prevalence of racism, popularity of extreme political and religious ideologies, etc.—campus ministry groups help guide the students through the confusing and tumultuous college years. Through fellowship and Bible studies, they provide Asian American students with psychological support, emotional comfort, and a community in which to grow their Christian faith. This trend continues even after their graduation, as many Asian American young adults look for their next "spiritual home" in English-speaking Asian American churches.

However, many Asian Americans discover that these campus ministry groups and Asian American churches, despite their good intentions and efforts, do not provide the coherent theological and ethical framework that young Asian Americans need in order to navigate the complex cultural and social environments that they experience. The prevailing theologies, ethics, and resources (both literary and personal) of these groups all too frequently end up being patterned after white evangelicalism, and pay little attention to the distinctive and complex cultural characteristics and struggles of Asian American Christians.

However, Asian American Christians, even if they share an evangelical commitment, are different from their white, African American, Native American, or Latino/a counterparts. Many are from immigrant families, with parents who continually drill them to study hard enough to gain entrance to a prestigious graduate/professional school or land a high-paying job. These Asian American young adults are often raised in a largely communal and hierarchical culture that conflicts with the current hyper-individualistic American culture. They inherit Asian religious or cultural traditions, etiquette, and practices, and grow up facing certain racial stereotypes and biases. Known as "the model minority," "the middleman minority," or "perpetual foreigners," Asian Americans experience marginalization in a culturally and socially distinctive way. Although many Americans think that Asian Americans are not discriminated against, sociological research clearly demonstrates the existence of various forms of racism against Asian Americans, including the "bamboo ceiling," the hypersexualization of the Asian female, and the misrepresentation of the Asian male in popular media.

In the midst of this turbulent sea of marginalizing experiences, cultural differences, dissonant social expectations, and family pressures, many Asian American young adults feel lost and unanchored. In addition, these young adults find that the faith of their parents is not relevant to their college and professional lives. Experiencing the radical discontinuity between their faith and the secular cultural ethos causes many to give up on Christianity and begin exploring other forms of spirituality.

This book is written to help Asian American young adults find a spiritual and moral framework for living faithfully and transformatively as Christians in a postmodern culture. Despite the remarkable growth of the Asian American population (including the increasing number of Asian American young adults) and of English-speaking Asian American congregations and campus ministries, there is still a lack of theological and ethical resources specifically written by and for Asian Americans with their distinctive spiritual and bi-cultural concerns in mind. This book hopes to be a voice of support, guidance, and edification for Asian American young adults by addressing various personal and social issues with which they struggle: identity, faith, marginality, parental relationships, community, personal vocation, sex, financial security, friendship/social networks, etc. Five different authors with rich and diverse ministry experience explore these complex issues based on serious sociological, ethical, and theological research.

It is the prayer of the authors that young Asian Americans find in this book valuable resources for integrating their faith and culture and for developing a coherent self-understanding that is deeply rooted in their identity as Christians.

This book would not have been possible without the support and prayers of many people. Our greatest thanks go to our family members. They have been our faithful company on this long journey and their love, care, and patience have been indispensable for the completion of this book.

We are indebted to many at Wipf and Stock Publishers—especially John Wipf and Jon Stock, the publishers, and Rodney Clapp, the editor—for their willingness to publish this book in service to Asian American Christian communities.

We are immensely grateful to Ken Fong for his passionate and faithful ministry to Asian American churches, and for his friendship with us. We are privileged to have his generous words of support in the foreword of this book. We also thank our schools, Fuller Theological Seminary and Azusa Pacific University, that supported our research and writing in various institutional forms.

Our deep appreciation goes to Matthew Jones, a Fuller PhD student, for his meticulous and careful work in proofreading, formatting, and compiling the manuscript.

We are equally thankful to G2G-KODIA Christian Education Center for their ministry to young Asian Americans (which, in fact, inspired this work) and their generous spiritual and moral support through meals and prayer.

It has been a long, tedious process to conceive and complete this book, but in the process we have come to know more about one another and have discovered that all of us are bound together by a love and passion for Asian American churches. Through a number of joyful fellowships in which we broke bread and shared our thoughts and personal stories, our friendship has grown. This is the fruit that we cherish and appreciate most in the blessed process of writing this book together!

INTRODUCTION

Hak Joon Lee

Jason is a twenty-two-year-old Chinese American living in LA. He has been quite distressed these days. After almost two years since his graduation from college, he still has not yet found a full-time job. Jason's mother wants him to go and get his MBA, but he has had enough with school and studying. Jason especially hates hearing his mom frequently compare him to David, his older brother, who is making good money as a computer engineer in New York. Jason has had several interviews in the advertising business, but to no avail. While searching for a job, he is now assisting his father's restaurant business as a store manager. He hates being perceived by customers as a FOB ("fresh off the boat") at the restaurant. To escape from all these stresses, he is spending more hours on SNS and online games, occasionally sneaking onto porn sites. Although online connection with his former college roommates and fraternity brothers gives him a temporary escape from his parents, he finds it difficult to candidly share what is really going on with his life.

Jason's parents keep asking Jason to join the English ministry service in their Chinese immigrant church where they are active, but Jason does not like the idea at all. Although he has grown up in the church, he does not want to associate with it any longer. The church seems socially isolated and culturally stagnant. Furthermore, attending the same church as his parents would be another reminder of his dependence on them. Rather, he has recently joined a newly planted Asian American church in the area where every Sunday about seventy people gather and worship. Jason was once very enthusiastic about faith, but that is no longer the case. Personally, God seems either indifferent to his prayers or powerless to help him find a job in this era of outsourcing, computerization, and AI. Socially, Jason feels the church is outdated on many social issues like politics, science, sexuality, etc. He mostly attends the church because he met Phillis, a young Indian American lady, there. He enjoys hanging out with her after worship, sometimes going for a walk or grabbing a drink. But his parents are not happy about it. They want him to find a Chinese girl, preferably from Taiwan or Hong Kong.

Jason feels lonely and frustrated, wondering when he is finally going to be independent from his parents, whether he even has a place in society, or whether he is indeed a loser.

This book is for young Asian American Christians like Jason who are struggling to figuring out who they are in the midst of radical cultural changes and colliding social forces. This book attempts to help them sort out what it means to be a young Asian American Christian today, and how to live their lives in a theologically faithful, culturally relevant, and personally meaningful way.

Young Asian American Christians! To comprehend this composite demographic designation is more complex than it appears because the four unique layers of identity—age, race, nationality, and religion—are bound up together in complex ways.[1] Because there is no guarantee that these four categories naturally cohere or are mutually balanced, it is not so easy to smoothly negotiate these layers of identities in one's life.[2] For example, there is a tension between "Asian" and "American." Asians have been historically victimized, treated as "perpetual foreigners" whose concerns and voices are easy to marginalize, even in conversations about racism. Such cultural tensions affect one's experience of age, too, as youth does not merit much respect or authority in Asian culture (although this is changing), while it is culturally celebrated and envied in the US. One does not see a necessary (or natural) association between being "Asian" and "Christian" (or "young" and "Christian") because Christianity in general has seldom been a predominant religion in Asia (although it is growing in Asia and among Asian Americans), and there is an increasing antipathy toward Christianity among Millennials. These tensions and fissures create confusion and fragmentation within a person. Consequently, many young Asian Americans

1. Their complexities exponentially increase when we add categories such as sex, gender, class, education, degree of assimilation (length of immigration), etc.

2. This means that depending on which component is emphasized, one's identity may have a different configuration.

struggle to reconcile these layers in their lives, and they often choose one or two categories over the rest (e.g., Asian over American or vice versa, Christian over Asian and/or American), reinforced under the pressure of living in a radically pluralistic society, often called postmodernity.

WHAT IS IDENTITY?

In approaching the complex challenges facing Asian American Christians, we begin with the question of "identity," examining its meaning, significance, and implications for them.

In general, identity is a coherent and sustaining sense of an individual or a group: who I am/who we are. In our common parlance in a postmodern celebration of individuality, self-construction, and expression, identity sounds like a completely individual phenomenon. However, although it is true that identity is personal, identity is not completely individualistic. Identity is a social phenomenon. As humans are social animals who cannot survive or fulfill their lives entirely removed from society, identity formation takes place in a particular social and cultural context as people interact with others. It is shaped relationally and contextually, through ongoing interactions between a person and his/her environments.

Identity is multifaceted and complex. We carry many identity labels. For example, I am a Christian, male, husband, heterosexual, father, son, brother, Asian American, Korean, scholar, teacher, baby boomer, co-president of a non-profit organization, and so on. Some labels (such as male, Asian American, Korean, father, son) are ascriptive, defined by passive membership and biological attributes/characteristics, while others are optional (voluntary), the result of social roles and professional positions that I have chosen.

Another important aspect of identity formation is its evolving nature; one's personal sense of identity is not fixed but matures through a slow yet steady process of differentiation, that is, growing beyond dependence on parents or guardians by gradually asserting oneself. Identity involves a constant search for balance between conviction and exploration, boundary and openness. We need a home base from which to explore the vast unknown universe. Differentiation requires inner strength—a sense of independence and self-confidence. Such inner strength could be aided by supportive groups, such as church youth groups, college campus fellowships, or fraternities or sororities that provide moral encouragement

3

and emotional care. To be successfully "differentiated" means a person can carry out and harmonize their multiple identity functions/labels with coherence and harmony.

Not every identity label is equally significant because we assign different importance and meaning to each label we carry. Figuring out how to negotiate and prioritize various identity labels is a major task in life. To mature as an adult means to come to terms with each of these labels and integrate them while deepening the meaning of each. Since identity is the seat of one's agency, a well-developed sense of identity provides a greater sense of focus, balance, and control in one's life because a person would have better discernment and direction. When a person does not have a good sense of identity, it is difficult to build true, intimate, meaningful relationships with others. A person of weak identity is likely to be defined by others or be overly defensive of himself/herself.

The question of identity has become far more acute, pressing, and complex in a postmodern, pluralistic society. Because of the highly fluid, mobile, instrumental nature of a social life, many individuals have become detached from close-knit communities (e.g., family, neighborhood, and church) and thus feel lonely, fragmented, and disoriented. Surrounded by competing ideologies, claims of allegiance, and shifting images, individuals feel confused and distracted. Many aspects of one's identity are no longer assumed to be "natural." In particular, ascriptive forms of identity are losing their powers to maintain the sense of coherent identity and become a huge burden for individuals in the midst of radical changes and shifts around oneself. This burden is far more pressing for young adults who are still in search of their identity and the meaning of life. The idea of "emerging adulthood," first introduced by Jeffrey Arnett in 2004,[3] discloses this blurred, ambiguous, transitory sense of identity that young adults experience in a postmodern society, which cannot provide shared moral frames of reference, stability of relationships, or secure jobs.

The label "emerging adults" refers to the young people aged eighteen to thirty as legal adults with physical maturity that have yet to achieve what has been traditionally associated with adults, such as marriage, a career, and a coherent value system (clear personal identity). As they feel unsettled between adolescence and adulthood, instability, uncertainty, and ambiguity characterize their emotional state. They are no longer adolescents, but they are not completely adults, either. They can drive, vote, and drink, but

3. Arnett, *Emerging Adulthood.*

4

they are not yet fully independent. Some still live with their parents. Either through their free choice or because of heightened professional competition in society, many aspects of their transition to adulthood are delayed: delayed completion of education (college and post-college), delayed career choice (or difficulty in finding a full-time job), and delayed marriage. With a heightened sense of self-awareness, they are trying to figure out who they are and what they really want to do.

CHALLENGES OF IDENTITY FOR ASIAN AMERICAN YOUNG ADULTS

This sense of transition, ambiguity, and tension that characterizes emerging adulthood is even more acute among Asian American emerging adults who live as a minority in the US. Like other emerging adults, young Asian Americans are still in transition, not yet settled on important personal matters such as friendship, love, work, and faith. In addition to this sense of unsettledness, they feel trapped between the two contrasting cultural forces of the East and the West. The gap between Asian and American cultures, negative social stereotypes ("model minority," "perpetual foreigner," etc.), generational discrepancies, and language barriers with their parents present enormous challenges for young Asian Americans. They feel pulled between Asian and American cultures, home and school, church and secular culture, usually without proper role models, caring mentors, or a reliable spiritual and moral framework to guide them.[4] Caught between two conflicting cultures and stuck in developmental transition, young Asian Americans undergo an intense inner struggle to find who they are and integrate their multiple and complex identities.

Countless young Christian Asian American adults feel socially unfit or marginalized in various ways. Some may be academically accomplished

---

4. The examples of these clashes include: the conflict between the ascriptive identity structure of immigrant churches vs. the fluid, individualistic, self-constructive experience of identity in the popular culture of the US; the frustration between the ambitious achievement of the orientation of Asian immigrants vs. the reality of racialized social norms and the bamboo ceiling; the tension between strong family values of chastity, purity, and sex roles vs. free, expressive, hypersexualized culture; the conflict between conservative evangelical ethics of immigrant churches vs. the liberal social ethos of campus and mainstream media (such as LGBTQ rights, environment, racial justice, etc.); financial security in the job search vs. the pursuit of individual creativity and desire for self-fulfillment; hierarchical patterns of sex roles vs. egalitarian self-expression.

but are socially underpowered and politically voiceless. Many feel disconnected or isolated even when they share physical spaces with their parents or other young adults for college and work. To avoid misunderstandings and conflicts, more often than not they hide their true feelings and emotions and hesitate to engage in genuine conversations outside their very close-knit circle of friends. This prolonged confusion, distress, and disorientation can result in depression, anxiety, alcohol and drug addiction, or even suicidal ideation and attempts.

This book responds to the spiritual struggles and emotional needs of young Asian American people experiencing cultural tensions, transition, in-between-ness, and ambiguity with the goal to help them develop a healthy, balanced, organic sense of identity on the basis of Christian faith that enables them to address the complex, multifaceted, and often conflicting aspects of their lives.

ASSUMPTIONS: FAITH AND IDENTITY

Overshadowed by the pressing concerns of work, love, and friends, the question of faith may appear secondary for emerging adults in general, and Asian American young adults in particular. Furthermore, in popular society, being Christian is no longer an attractive idea. Christianity is dismissed as little more than a source of social prejudice and intolerance. Some young adults may occasionally participate in worship activities without assigning much social significance.

Despite the cultural suspicion of institutionalized religion, however, faith (or spirituality), in a broad sense, remains an important factor for emerging adults as they develop their own "worldview and faith stance amid a wide array of competing perspectives."[5] During this period, some young adults assess and reevaluate their faith by asking, "are the values and beliefs of my faith relevant and worth keeping?" Some give up their faith and look for other options, while others reclaim and recommit themselves to faith.

It is the premise of this book that, contrary to popular perception, the question of faith is central to one's identity formation and development, and Christian faith is well-equipped with resources to address various issues related to identity. As identity constitutes a sense of one's uniqueness (or particularity) and arises in relationships with significant others (God,

5. Setran and Kiesling, *Spiritual Formation of Emerging Adulthood*, 1.

parents, siblings, friends, romantic partners, community), God ought to be understood as the most significant source of identity in one's life.

Our relationship with God offers the identity that is antecedent to any other identities.[6] Just as being married changes a person's identity (with a new sense of responsibility, security, and joy), entering into a relationship with God[7] changes our identity—a change that permanently marks our lives with a more profound sense of meaning, purpose, and selfhood.

Faith in God has meaning-making power for one's life. Faith (our relationship with God) helps organize and coordinate the multiple, complex, often competing aspects of our social roles. Christian faith ought to address the various dimensions of identity in a coherent, empowering, and plausible manner. For example, the Christian confession of the triune God—the creator, redeemer, and fulfiller—touches various crucial aspects of our identity development and maturation. God the creator is involved in our identity development as the source and the origin of our life (Ps 139); God the redeemer describes the loving God who unconditionally embraces and forgives us; God the fulfiller is the one who accompanies, guides, and protects us in our journey toward a deep, meaningful, and fulfilled life in a community. This triune God (who is three in one, one in three) anchors our lives in redemptive love and friendship. Thanks to this complex and dynamic God, Christianity takes a holistic and balanced approach to identity by engaging the question of "*who* I am" in relation to "*whose* I am" (first God, then parents and culture), "*whom* I share my life with" (family, friends, and community), and "*where* I am going" (meaning, purpose, and direction such as vocation and the common moral cause in the kingdom of God).[8]

Furthermore, the question of identity is central to Christianity. In fact, God's name YHWH (Exod 3:14) in Hebrew, meaning "I Am Who I Am," implies God's strong and ongoing presence in history and also that God is the one who causes things to be. This name was revealed to Moses when he demanded to know God's personal name before he decided to accept God's call to deliver the Israelites from the bondage of Egypt. Hence the name YHWH also serves as the designator (identity) of a God who is the

---

6. See May, *Testing the National Covenant*, 83.

7. Covenant is a biblical term that describes this relationship that is personal, intimate, experiential, and ongoing in nature.

8. Jill M. Johnson, "Identity and Faith," http://www.ministrymatters.com/all/entry/5383/identity-and-faith.

deliverer or liberator of the oppressed. Similarly, for example, the idea of election expressed in numerous places in the Bible ("a chosen race, a royal priesthood, a holy nation, God's own people" [1 Pet 2:9]) speaks of the deep biblical concern with identity.

God is concerned with the identity development of God's people. Many stories in the Bible are associated with the formation and maturing of identity rooted in relationship with God. When Abram was ninety-nine years old, God gave new names to Abram and Sarai, i.e., new identities that matched with their initial callings (Gen 12:1–3): *Abraham*, a father of many nations (Gen 17:5) and *Sarah*, a mother of nations (Gen 17:15–16). Similarly, Jacob encountered God in the middle of the night on his way to return home after twenty years of service to his uncle, Laban; he wrestled with God and succeeded, receiving a new name, *Israel* (the one who struggles with God). The Israelites' life in the wilderness was a process of being reborn as a priestly kingdom free from all the destructive effects of their slavery in Egypt. This identity-granting (transforming) act of God continues in the New Testament. For example, Simon, a fisherman, received the name Peter (which means "rock") from Jesus. The above examples show that identity is an integral aspect of Christian faith and that, far from being static, dogmatic, or defensive, faith does not arrest our development but guides us to a deeper, more mysterious appreciation of life in God.

In a Christian moral framework, which is relational, faith is rooted in an identity that arises from relationship with God and others. When faith is not rooted in identity, it becomes little more than an accessory no matter how long one has been a Christian and attended the church. In the final analysis, faith is the operative work (*modus vivendi*) of our identity as the children of God, exercised in every realm of our lives. Faith is the expression of who I am/we are in my/our relationship with God and others. Detached from identity (personal and cultural), faith is likely to wither away or be discarded. Faith is not something external to the self that we put on and put off (like a jacket) at certain occasions (e.g., rituals), but part and parcel of our very selves.

THE ORDER OF THE BOOK

This book theologically addresses the issues that most intimately and immediately affect Asian American youths' sense of identity: God, race, family, sex, gender, friendship, money, vocation, the model minority myth, and community. Obviously most of these issues (except the model minority myth) are what other emerging young adults are also wrestling with regardless of their racial/ethnic backgrounds; however, this book engages these issues uniquely and consistently from the contexts of Asian American young adult life.

The first chapter addresses the question of God. With an incisive observation of how Asian cultural baggage can often hijack or cloud biblical images and themes, it takes the ideas of relational legalism and filial piety as hidden cultural forces that distort Asian American Christians' images of God. As an alternative, the author proposes imaging God as a Lover to challenge a suffocating duty-orientation and to discover how joy and delight are at the heart of Christian faith.

Challenging a conventional, dichotomous approach to the East-West cultural divide, chapter 2 lays out a way to understand culture in its full complexity and nuance: there aren't just good and bad aspects of culture, but the good comes with a shadow side and the bad is often redeemable. The chapter then applies this complex assessment of culture to family-centric Asian values that influence the parent-child relationship offering a more nuanced and careful guide on how to discern our discipleship to Christ as we interact with our parents.

Chapter 3 discusses the topic of friendship and social networking that occupies the central place of social life for emerging young adults. Relying on social scientific and psychological studies on the impact of SNSs on identity and well-being, the chapter explores the significance of SNSs on Asian American identity formation, together with the strengths and liabilities of distinctively Asian American friendship network formation and operation.

Chapter 4 engages with the stewardship of money. As the Asian American population and their financial resources grow in the United States, Asian Americans are increasingly becoming the target of corporations and cultural entities. This chapter asks readers to critically examine the patterns of consumption that young Asian Americans have inherited from their families and the significant role that their material consumption plays for their personal identity. It invites the readers to reflect on the importance of stewarding their consumption patterns for the common good, and the biblical idea of creation theology is employed to anchor the notion of the common good in the foundation of creation as well as the *eschaton*.

Distinguishing the Christian idea of vocation from a career or job, chapter 5 explores how God calls Christians to be agents of hope, blessing, and reconciliation anywhere and everywhere we go, irrespective of what we do for a living. It claims that discerning our vocation involves listening to the needs of the world while also listening to who we are as God-made individuals, which as Asian Americans, requires that we recognize the ways in which our familial and social relationships and expectations come to bear on our self-understanding of vocation.

Chapter 6 studies the racial identity that Asian Americans experience. For Asian American young adults, racial identity formation is necessary but complex and challenging as they live between two starkly different, long-standing cultures of Asia and America (because of the tribalistic tendency of the former and the racist history of the latter). Borrowing insights from social psychology and cultural studies, this chapter studies how Asian Americans can creatively come to terms with their racial identity in the triune God, without suppressing or absolutizing their Asianness and Americanness.

Chapter 7 dives into sexuality, the taboo subject among most Asian Americans families. Despite the rampant exposure of sexuality in the popular media, Asian American Christian families rarely talk about sexuality as they rigidly hold onto conservative sexual ethics of Asian culture and evangelical Christianity that emphasize the purity, chastity, and holiness of sexuality. Taking into account a growing gap between the promiscuous aspects of culture and the traditional sexual ethics of Asian American evangelical churches, the chapter explores biblically grounded and reflective sexual ethics based on a covenantal paradigm of friendship informed by the Gospel of John that stresses faithfulness, mutuality, and self-sacrifice.

Chapter 8 begins with the assumption that gender identity is socially constructed. For Asian Americans, the pernicious double influence of the male-dominated hierarchy of Asian culture and gendered stereotypes of conservative evangelical Christianity in the US, have a malforming effect on gender identities and roles. In light of Genesis 1–2 and Galatians 3, this chapter offers a liberative, non-essentialized, hybrid sense of gender identity in which Asian Americans can structure and restructure their gender identities as an alternative to a rigid, bifurcated view based on gendered roles.

Chapter 9 addresses the perils and pitfalls involved in the "myth of the model minority." Debunking the misleading claims and potential harms of the idea of the model minority, this chapter challenges readers to be critical of the model minority narrative and be sensitive to the ways in which this narrative plays out in the social discourse and relationships between racial/ethnic minority groups. It invites Asian Americans to live as people formed into the image of Christ, not as people formed in the image of the model minority stereotype, and it encourages them toward compassion, righteousness, and a life spent in solidarity with others.

Finally, chapter 10 examines Christian ideas about community and its practices in Asian American contexts. Although more and more Asian Americans gather among themselves to meet their cultural and emotional needs, they still struggle to build good Christian communities because their efforts are motivated by their resentment toward Asian immigrant communities and their marginalization in white dominant society. This chapter explores the biblical idea of covenant as an organizing method of building an enduring community based on trust, justice, and compassion. Using Daniel and his friends as an example, it asks what a covenantal community of Asian Americans would look like where Asian Americans not only find personal comfort and encouragement, but also pursue a higher moral cause such as racial justice and other community issues relevant to them.

In discussing the identity of young Asian American Christians, this book attempts to approach it in a balanced way, paying close attention to the four central aspects of their demographic identity: young, Asian, American, and Christian. In approaching a specific topic, each chapter opens with a story of Asian American cultural experiences before proceeding to identify major contributing factors and important theological and cultural issues that Asian American young adults face in distinctively Asian American contexts. Then each chapter addresses these issues from a biblical and theological perspective, concluding with key discussion questions that invite the readers into further reflection and conversation.

The book takes a dialogical approach. The authors of this book have many years of diverse ministry experiences (in local churches and campuses) with Asian Americans, and engage Asian American Christian identity in its multifaceted complexity, with special attention to the core issues/relationships arising from postmodern cultural contexts. One could use this book in several different ways, but it is ideal for a small group setting where members can share their struggles, challenges, and hopes with others in personal and informal ways.

In addressing these issues, the authors have made every effort to be socially attentive and culturally inclusive, for all Asian American groups in our context. However, as cultural contexts extensively vary from person to person (depending on immigration status, regional ties, family backgrounds, etc.) readers may not agree with every observation or claim that we make. Some chapters may resonate closely with your backgrounds, and others may not. This is normal! Asian Americans are the most culturally and religiously diverse demographic group in the US.[9] Because of this heterogeneity, it is almost impossible to offer a unified theological and ethical framework that addresses Asian American issues in a comprehensive way. We have tried our best to be inclusive, but we also acknowledge that some examples are more attentive to East Asian Americans due to our own ethnic backgrounds as well as the sheer size of the Asian American population from the region.

It is the prayer of the authors that this book be used to help young Asian Americans think about Christian faith in their own life contexts so that they find their own reasons to believe and claim Christian faith as their own, and that they might flourish and thrive in this land for the glory of God's kingdom.

9. "Asian" refers to the people descended from Asia, which is the largest, most populous continent, home to a vast array of cultures and world religions.

1

GOD

Daniel D. Lee

" That would be hell." This is what a young Korean American man said at a retreat when we were talking about how heaven would be a place where we will be with God all the time forever. Before this conversation, I had suggested that we might imagine God as someone like our father and that heaven would be like spending all eternity with God in the same room. My point was that whether we are aware of it or not, we often do think of God as someone like our earthly father or mother. The puzzling aspect of this young man's faith was that he would say that he still "loved" God. However, this "love" was the same love with which he loved his father. Over the years, I have talked to so many young Asian Americans who assure me of their "love" for their fathers and mothers, but do not "like" them, nor associate them with joy or pleasure. Their filial "love" was more about honoring, respecting, and being dutiful. With this kind of "love" much can be accomplished, i.e., commitment, obedience, and maybe even sacrifice. And yet, all that would fall short of the kind of genuine covenant interaction God is seeking with us.

For many Asian American Christians this idea of loving God, but not liking him, is often inevitable if this dynamic also characterizes their relationship with their parents.[1] Our earliest relational attachments become

---

1. Rizzuto's research shows that our images of God are profoundly and yet implicitly impacted by our parent figures. Rizzuto, *Birth of the Living God.*

patterns and templates for our intimate relationships for the rest of our lives, unless we are able to consciously revise them.[2] This chapter focuses on some of the problematic aspects of our cultural matrix that impact our closest relationships as well as our thoughts about God. While I refer to parental relationships here, chapter 5 will examine the topic of parents more extensively.

It seems as though the easy solution for this God representation problem would be to correct or replace false images with biblically and theologically informed ones. However, these familial images are much more deeply ingrained and difficult to unseat, even impacting our scriptural interpretation and theological reflection, especially if we cannot precisely name them. We can talk about God loving us and us loving God, but even these words can be understood in a different light. All this is happening mostly unconsciously with well-meaning people, even pastors and ministry leaders. We are talking about how culture impacts the gospel. Culture runs deep, just as blood is thicker than water.

The idea of a cultural captivity of the gospel has been around since the Reformation, when Martin Luther declared a "Babylonian captivity" of the church.[3] Luther used this term in his attacks against distorted views and uses of the sacraments, but later theologians began using it to describe how culture domesticates and distorts the gospel. In fact, no context is immune to these distortions and they occur continually because we always try to tame God for our own purposes, knowingly or unknowingly.

Recently, many missional theologians began reflecting how the Western, and more specifically American culture, has unwittingly subverted the gospel.[4] What these theologians named as virulent forces, such as consumerism and privatization of faith, for example, applies in general to Asian Americans as well. However, as Asian Americans, our faith is also influenced and impacted by our Asian cultural heritage. These Asian cultural, religious, and philosophical heritages are part of Asian American lives, in

---

2. See Siegel, *Developing Mind.*

3. Luther, "The Babylonian Captivity of the Church, 1520," in *Luther's Works,* vol. 36, 3–126.

4. Newbigin has been instrumental in articulating this Western captivity, that the Christian West is really post-Christian and more pagan then we assume it to be. Newbigin, *Foolishness to the Greeks.* Hauerwas develops this captivity idea and focus more on the confusion of American civil religion with the gospel. Hauerwas and Willimon, *Resident Aliens.*

varying ways and degrees, whether we are conscious of it or not.[5] They are often the deepest parts of us, distant and perhaps primal parts that many of us have no words to describe. This is true even when some Asian Americans would like to abandon or repress their Asianness so they can fit in better and be accepted as "real" Americans.

Before we continue, it is crucial to note that we are not honing in on Asian heritage because of its seemingly foreign and "pagan" nature.[6] That kind of attitude would be falling victim to the pervasive Orientalism that still exists in our society, an ideology that portrays Asian culture as backwards, exotic, or grotesque. As we proceed, we must presuppose that there are redemptive elements present in every culture, American or Asian of various sorts, as well as distortions and perversions of God's gift of good creation. For example, we can point to the Japanese aesthetic of *wabi-sabi,* in which beauty is found in imperfection. The art of *kintsugi,* which mends broken pottery with gold, expresses this surprising beauty. This might serve as an analogy for God's redemptive grace. Or we might contemplate how the Korean cultural notion of *han,* defined as deep unresolved resentment and helplessness, could expand the doctrine of sin with its deep insights into the sticky and structural nature of human brokenness.[7] While an extended discussion of culture is beyond the scope of this chapter, I provide these examples to clarify that the problematic aspects of Asian heritage are not definitive of the whole.[8] Given this important caveat, cultural distortions of the gospel are real and must be addressed, whether they arise from Western culture or from various Asian heritages.

We begin by noting that there is no simple panacea for this problem of cultural distortion, because our cultural context is all-pervasive; we are surrounded like fish in water. Our only hope is to become aware of this murky water that we are swimming in and ask God's guidance and correction again and again. Theologian Darrell Guder describes this process of divine critique and correction as a continuing conversion from culture's

---

5. Nadeau shows ways in which Asian heritages are communicated, transmitted, and expressed as cultural practices and expressions. Nadeau, *Asian Religions.*

6. Asian heritage should not be considered entirely non-Christian. For many South Indian Americans, such as those of Malayalam heritage, their Asian heritage includes the Mar Thoma Syrian Church, a rich tradition of two thousand years.

7. See Park's *The Wounded Heart of God.*

8. See this article for a more developed theology of culture to engage Asian cultural roots. Daniel Lee, "Cultural Archetypes."

gospel truncations.[9] We need to be converted by God's Word over and over again to be faithful. We never really grasp the gospel fully and completely until we see God face to face.

So, getting back to knowing a God whom we enjoy loving, we turn to what an Asian American cultural captivity might look like.

WHAT KIND OF GOD?

John Calvin begins his famous *Institutes* by saying that the knowledge of ourselves and knowledge of God are intertwined.[10] When we know God, we truly know ourselves. Our identity is found in God, but what is our God really like? Having a true knowledge of God is more difficult than it sounds, even for those who grew up in church, because this knowledge is not about what we profess to believe. Rather, the knowledge that matters is the one out of which we live.

For example, a simple spiritual exercise can reveal this discrepancy between our professed faith and implicit faith. In their edited collection, *Devotional Classics*, Richard Foster and James Bryan Smith recommend fasting from spiritual disciplines:

> Abandon your spiritual disciplines for one week. While this may seem like a radical exercise, it may serve to free you from several hidden demons, such as the performance trap, pride in your spiritual works, religious addiction, and the judging of those who do less than you. Use the time to relax and enjoy God.[11]

Initially this experience appears puzzling or even dangerous. What would being a Christian mean if we did not read the Bible, pray, or go to church? We can add here ministry responsibilities and roles as well. However, there is deep wisdom in this fast from spiritual disciplines, because so often we confuse godliness with God. The point of spiritual practices is to open ourselves up to God's presence, encountering God in and through these acts. In other words, they are tools, a means to an end. They are not meaningful in and of themselves, because then they could become idols replacing God. Without this reminder, these practices can become terrible

---

9. Guder, *Continuing Conversion*. Guder's book *Missional Church* actually played a key role in coining the popular but often misunderstood term "missional."

10. Calvin, *Institutes*, 35.

11. Foster and Smith, *Devotional Classics*, 39.

tyrants oppressing us with their demands of spiritual performance. Richard Foster warns that our spiritual disciplines can turn into "soul-killing laws . . . [that] breathe death."[12]

Martin Luther says that without knowing the gracious God revealed in Christ, our God can be a demon who demands obedience, while threatening punishment and hell. Luther was talking about Christians, not unbelievers, whose God functioned like a devil that we fear.[13] This is the God that we believe we have to *love*, but do not *like* or even secretly *hate*.

This is why church, ironically, can be a perfect place to miss God. Why? Because there are so many spiritual, godly activities in church that we can so easily substitute for God. We can actually miss the living God and get sidetracked by godliness. Diabolically speaking, what could be simpler, but absolutely detrimental, than confusing God with spiritual activities? Of course, the Bible has plenty of examples of God judging his people for their misguided "godliness," such as fasting, worship, and other spiritual practices (Isa 58; Amos 5:21–23; Matt 23). With these godly idols, many will never notice what has happened, and others might even be encouraged or impressed by our fixation on these practices. Since learning this rather frightening insight, I have recommended this fast to many young Asian American Christians and these are the responses I have received:

On the one hand, there are those who cannot do it. Tom said that the first couple of days of this fast were fine, but after the third day of not praying or reading the Bible, he began to get scared, afraid that God was going to "get him" for disobeying. So he stopped his fast and got back to his disciplines. Now, Tom had never been all that regular with his spiritual disciplines to begin with, but the idea of consciously and actively abandoning them for a time filled him with divine terror. In a way, Tom had been using these disciplines as a way to "protect" himself from God, so God would not "get him" for being bad. Of course, his reasoning begs the question of just how much he would have to do to "protect" himself from God's wrath or correction. Two hours of daily prayer? Ten chapters of daily Scripture reading? Was all that merely out of fear? More importantly, just what kind of a God is this?

On the other hand, there are those who love this fast. They say if it is okay with God for them not to do spiritual disciplines or ministry work,

12. Foster, *Celebration of Discipline*, 9.

13. Barth, *Church Dogmatics* IV/1, 415–16. Barth refers to Luther's sermons on the Gospel of John.

they would *never* do it. They never struggled with legalism anyways, but rather with antinomianism. It turns out that they never understood the point of these practices to begin with. And tasting freedom from them, they are not sure if they would ever go back to doing them. John confessed that he never enjoyed spiritual disciplines, that they were always just chores that God seemed to want from him. Never enjoyed spending time with God? Never took pleasure in encountering God in worship or service? Again, what kind of a God does he believe in?

RELATIONAL LEGALISM AND CHEAP GRACE

As Asian American Christians, we are particularly vulnerable to this theological struggle because of our Asian heritage, especially Confucianism. According to a Confucian worldview, the universe is controlled by a moral principle. So, at the heart of the universe is not a loving person, but a law. Given this worldview, our lives become a matter of duty and constant striving to study and follow the law. Within this framework, the idea of God being our father does not necessarily help either. Theologian Jung Young Lee says that his Korean father was the embodiment of law and order within his family.[14] This embodiment of the cosmic moral principle explains the archetype of Asian fathers as being stoic, stern disciplinarians.[15] There are similar motifs within Hinduism. One of the significant Hindu deities, Shiva, in a way serves a father archetype because he and his consort Parvati are the only gods that have children. Shiva as a father is generally austere and aloof. And, of course, there is that incident where he cuts off his son Ganesha's head and replaces it with an elephant's head. These kinds of mythological stories inform cultural imagination as they are told and retold. In that vein, the father in Indian culture is traditionally "an overtly emotionally distant disciplinarian who formulates and embodies the ideals of the family."[16]

14. Jung Young Lee, *Trinity*, 147.

15. The distinction between *archetypes* versus *stereotypes* is helpful here. In how I am using these terms, a stereotype is a generalization about cultural values or traits, i.e., Asian fathers are emotionally aloof. These might be true of your family, or they might not be. On the other hand, an archetype is a specific pattern or idea that has a particular religious or ideological heritage, like this Confucian idea of a father. Not all Asian fathers are like this, but this idea of fatherhood, even in its watered down and implicit expressions, has significant influence as the cultural heritage of Asians and Asian Americans. See Daniel Lee, "Cultural Archetypes."

16. Roland, *Cultural Pluralism*, 138.

Relationship with this father who embodies the law can be defined as a legalistic relationship or as a form of *relational legalism*.[17] We often hear that Christianity is not a religion, but a relationship. However, as you can see here, if some relationships can be *legalistic*, characterized by rules and requirements, then there is really no difference between religion and relationship. In this sense, faith ultimately is all about the fulfillment of our duty to a demanding authority figure. Therefore, talking about God as a father, even a loving father, does not necessarily save us from this *relational legalism*.

What has happened with this distorted view of our relationship with God is that God's law has become separated and autonomous from God revealed in Christ. Dietrich Bonhoeffer says that this is why the Pharisees could not understand Jesus and fought against his teaching about the law.[18] To these religious leaders, the law itself became deified; the law was God. In his ministry, Jesus rejects this idolatry and returned the law back under God's reign. It wasn't that the law was bad. Rather, it needed to come under God's lordship and become again a divine instrument of grace.

To be sure, it is possible to deify grace as well. Bonhoeffer's idea of cheap grace is well known.[19] What Bonhoeffer called out was the abstraction of the idea of grace, separating it from a living God. Perhaps some might say that this is just as prevalent as legalism these days, or maybe even more, but two words of caution about thinking this way: First, we should be very clear that we are not talking about the problem of too much grace, because there is no such thing. True grace never makes anyone lazy, although it might lead those who have been oppressed by a distorted view of God and law towards a much-needed time of rest and restoration. The Apostle Paul was captivated by Christ's overwhelming grace and his discipleship was marked by joyful commitment. Second, there is no need for a balance between law and grace; there is no such thing either because it is grace and grace alone that saves us and motivates us to love and fulfill the law. The law serves as a signpost for the Christian discipleship, not the source.

Grace must be *God's* grace and not just a warm and fuzzy idea or feeling. Grace must be predicated upon the very being of God. Otherwise, it

17. This relational legalism is not exclusive to fathers. While the rest of this chapter continues with the language of fathers, they serve as stand-ins for mothers or other parental authority figures as well.

18. Bonhoeffer, *Discipleship*, 117.

19. Bonhoeffer, *Discipleship*, 43.

may turn into another principle, as the idea of cheap grace functions for many evangelicals today. In a sense, grace is a way to understand God, or a commentary on who God is. And God's laws are expressions of divine grace and love as well.[20] How else would the psalmist love the law and consider it sweeter than honey (Ps 119:103)? Delighting in the law as an expression of God's love is the only way to truly obey in a biblical sense.

CHRIST'S SACRIFICE AS A BURDEN?

Along with this *relational legalism, filial piety* could also distort the gospel. As we noted, many Asian Americans suffer from a spirituality that is oriented towards the fulfillment of duty. For example, Confucian tradition in general is organized in terms of duty fulfillment. This is not necessarily negative, because duty fulfillment has its rightful place within family and society. However, this duty orientation also has a shadow side of shame. Here are some examples: If you want to be a good parent and not bring shame upon yourself and your family, you fulfill your duty by sacrificing for your children. If you want to be a good child and not bring shame upon yourself and your family, you fulfill your duty by sacrificing for your parents. This idea of being a good child is what filial piety means, and parental sacrifice is the other side of this coin.

Applying this idea to the Asian American context, think of the immigrant parent who has come to America, maybe working in excruciating conditions for their children. Their sacrifice demands that their children respond in obedience, sacrifice, and outstanding academic achievement. This linking of parental sacrifice and filial piety means that the love of parents is not necessarily free. It is part of a social contract. This contractual aspect is why some parents act as though the career choices of their children are part of an unspoken agreement. The children provide meaning, prestige, and even later retirement care to the parents. Again, this does not necessarily have to be negative, although it can turn toxic.

The cross of Christ could be misinterpreted in this duty-orientation as something like a great parental sacrifice, which requires a reciprocal response of filial piety. The greater the sacrifice, the greater the debt of filial piety, which means that the message of God's grace becomes a source of

---

20. Karl Barth argues that law should be thought of as a form of the gospel. Rightly understood, God's commands are good news because they are given to give us life. See Barth, "Gospel and Law," in *Community, State and Church,* 71–100.

burden, not freedom. If Christ's sacrifice is not really free, but obligates a reciprocating response, it becomes the most oppressive message with God-sized expectations. Of course, the good news is that the blessing of Christ's sacrifice is truly free, but in light of that reality, many Asian American Christians need to figure out their motivation for obedience, worship, and service, other than obligation and duty.

GOD THE LOVER

Regarding this troubling phenomena of relating to God in terms of dreadful duty even while "loving" God, a pastor friend shared a question that her church member asked. In all earnestness, this person asked her, "Pastor, what is the minimum that I should do as a Christian?" In other words, "How do I make sure that I avoid hell, without overdoing it, like earning a mansion in heaven? I want to enjoy this life as much as possible, but not lose my ticket to heaven by making God angry." Sometimes our parents have many demands and expectations, but we can still be considered faithful children without overdoing it as long as we do not totally fail. His question of the minimum duty might be an idea that people think about, but if he knew how problematic it was, he might have been too ashamed to ask it. Using father imagery, especially with our Asian thinking about fathers, obscures how ridiculous the question is, because in terms of duty, we can *love* our parents as we should, but not *like* them freely and joyously.

This is why, for Asian Americans, this father God image is a double-edged sword. It resonates so profoundly sometimes, but its emotional baggage can be onerous. We need to redeem God as Father, the true Father like no human father can ever be, because this analogy is vital to our faith. However, since the Bible uses many different images for God, we will benefit from using others. Thinking about God as Father will only get us so far, because like all the other biblical analogies for God, it has its limits.

For example, if we think about God as Lover then certain spiritual truths become clearer.[21] Thinking about God as Lover can sound strange to many Asian American Christians, but this is a prominent image of God in the Bible and throughout church history as well. This lover image is connected to divine beauty that is often ignored or overshadowed by truth and

---

21. This is not the same as the reductive and individualistic "Jesus is my boyfriend" kind of spirituality. God the Lover is still the God of the kingdom, who rules over all and calls us to lives of discipleship.

goodness.[22] Whereas the truth of God leads us to believe, and the goodness of God convicts us to be good, the beauty of God woos us to love. Joy, pleasure, desire, beauty, and delight are all central to the gospel, however, we cannot get there by narrowly focusing on duty or obedience.

So returning to the question above about doing the minimum, what if I asked my wife, "Honey, what is the minimum that I should do to be a faithful husband?" or basically, "What can I get away with, and still be considered faithful to you, still be your husband?" Now, it is much clearer why the "minimum" question is not one that a Christian would ask, just like any husband worth his salt would never ask such a question.

Using this lover image for God, thinking about any spiritual act toward God as duty makes little sense. What if I told you that even though I don't enjoy it, it is my duty to spend time connecting with my wife every day, and go on a date with her once a week? What if I forced myself to do them even though I dreaded them because she might get upset with me? What if I secretly wished that I never had to do them? Now, if I said that, you would say that something is fundamentally wrong with my marriage.[23]

Of course, all this is not true. I do not think this way about my time with my wife. I, in fact, love my wife, and love loving her as well. And I know that the true end of spending time with my wife is enjoying that time. It has very little to do with trying to be a good husband, even though that has its place. In that same way, if being a Christian is to actually encounter the beauty of God and to be enraptured by it, then we simply cannot settle for duty alone. We would know that the point of obeying God is that we get to obey God, or that we have the pleasure of following God's heart in our obedience. We would know that the point of worshiping God is that we get to worship God, the one we love with great pleasure. The point of serving others is that we get to encounter God in the people that we serve. Discipleship would mean losing our lives to gain the pearl of great price, our beautiful Savior. Missions, evangelism, and seeking kingdom justice would be delights and joys when we are pursuing this God and God's divine

---

22. Hans Urs von Balthasar, a German theologian, bemoans how truth and goodness have been stressed at the expense of God's beauty in modern theology. Thus he seeks to vigorously rectify this problem with his seven-volume masterpiece on theological aesthetics. Balthasar, *Glory of the Lord*, Volume 1, 9.

23. John Piper, who is popular among many Asian American Christians, presses this point about delight in his book *Desiring God*, but does not adequately acknowledge the dangers of duty. Duty in abstraction can be spiritually lethal. Piper, *Desiring God*.

reign over all.[24] Christian life would not necessarily be easier, but how we think about sacrifices would be very different. If you have ever been in love with someone, such sacrifices in that relationship take on a very different meaning. And when these acts begin to lose their meaning, self-loathing is not a response that will lead towards renewed obedience. No, I need to remind myself of God's beauty again, to be reminded of the joy and delight in this Person, which is the true motivation of all that we do.

According to the book of Revelation, the ultimate meaning of the universe is found in a wedding:

> I saw the Holy City, the new Jerusalem, coming down out of heaven from God, prepared as a bride beautifully dressed for her husband. And I heard a loud voice from the throne saying, "Now the dwelling of God is with men, and he will live with them. They will be his people, and God himself will be with them and be their God . . . (Rev 21:2–3)

That phrase about us being God's people and God being our God is covenantal talk, describing the nature of our relationship. Interestingly, this language is also found in the Song of Songs, in a lover's relationship with his beloved (Song 2:16; 6:3). This is the language of deep, intimate love. God is after a deep, intimate, and committed relationship with us, in which we belong to God and God belongs to us. This is the meaning of creation and the purpose of the universe.

TALKING BACK AND GENUINE COVENANT INTERACTION

Using this language of "lover" and "covenant" changes our relational dynamic with God. God is not just an authority figure to be obeyed no matter what. Doubt, protest, and lament are all integral to biblical faith, although they are contrary to much of Asian heritage and the evangelical culture of unquestioned submission. God invites us to, at times, faithfully challenge and dissent. Of course, we should not do this flippantly. However, when life makes no sense, it is a matter of faithfulness to know that God is bigger than our anger, disappointment, frustration, and doubt, and that we can "talk back" to God.

---

24. Newbigin thought that making missions a duty made it a burden and missed the New Testament evidence that shows missions as "a kind of explosion of joy." Newbigin, *Gospel*, 116.

Take Job, for example. Contrary to popular misunderstandings (including a worship song), Job does not stop at saying "He gives and takes away. Blessed be the name of the Lord."[25] Job "talks back" to God on and on over thirty chapters. And in the end, God considered Job to be speaking truth about God, unlike his friends who believed Job's protest to be impious.

What is our God like? Does our view of God guide us towards a genuine covenant interaction or merely coercive obedience? Old Testament scholar Walter Brueggemann contends that without lament we lose a "genuine covenant interaction" with God because we are reduced to "'yes-men and women' from whom 'never is heard a discouraging word.'"[26] Brueggemann contends that in this kind of relationship ultimately

> [the] believer is nothing, and can praise or accept guilt uncritically where life with God does not function properly. The outcome is a "False Self," bad faith that is based in fear and guilt and lived out as resentful or self-deceptive works of righteousness. The absence of lament makes a religion of coercive obedience the only possibility.[27]

The kind of relationships that God had with God's closest friends in the Bible are often confrontational, i.e. Abraham, Jacob, Moses, and Jeremiah. This is the reason why God's people are named "Israel," which means "one who wrestles with God," which is quite an odd name. Why not one who surrenders and submits to God? God is not satisfied with just obedience or submission. Rather, God is after love, and not the kind of love with which we began this chapter, but joyous, delightful, desirable love. That is the only way eternity with God makes any sense.

This chapter gave examples of cultural captivity in the Asian American Christian context. When I was younger, I used to think that if I could get all these so-called "pagan" Asian heritages like Confucianism, Buddhism, Taoism, and Hinduism out of my faith, then it would be pure. However, such thinking, rooted in a cultural Orientalism, can result in self-fragmentation. Trying to take Asian heritage out of myself is a hopeless endeavor, and not a very helpful or healthy one.

There are others who believe that escaping to a white or multicultural church will solve the problem of cultural captivity. However, as stated above,

25. Redman and Redman, "Blessed Be Your Name."

26. Brueggemann, *Psalms*, 102.

27. Brueggemann, *Psalms*, 103–4.

American culture, with its Western heritage, domesticates and distorts the gospel in its own fashion.[28] Also, the problem with escaping to a non-Asian American church is that we are still taking ourselves with us, us with all our cultural heritage. No matter where we go, we need to deal with these issues because they are part of who we are, just like our family background and physical features.

God is after us, desiring to satisfy us with divine love so that our lives may be characterized by joy and gladness (Ps 90:14). Is this the God that we really believe in, a God that we love and like? Are we captivated by God's love or are we subjugating God under our cultural heritage?

DISCUSSION QUESTIONS:

1. Ask your Christian friends why they obey God and if they like obeying God. What is their motivation? What drives their spiritual lives? Ask them if they ever wonder about what "the minimum" is that they should do as a Christian.

2. Why do you think that the greatest commandment is to *love* the Lord, instead of obey the Lord, worship the Lord, or submit to the Lord? Meditate upon what God is desiring from us.

3. Do you think you would be more scared to fast from spiritual disciplines, or would you want the fast to never end? Try fasting from spiritual disciplines for a week or two in order to make sure that they have not become idols replacing God. While you fast, remind yourself of God's delight in you because of Christ. Hopefully at the end of the fast, you'll miss the spiritual disciplines because they are ways to connect with our beautiful God.

4. Reflect upon your image of God. Do you *like* God? Do you *trust* God? This exercise is not about knowing the right answer. Ask God to reveal what is really in your heart. Often we try to hide our negative thoughts of God from God, but this is not how biblical spirituality works. The Psalms contain all these raw and messy emotions about life and even disappointments about God as prayers. We can learn what true and honest prayer looks like by learning from them. Ask God to lead you to be deeply honest before God.

28. Rah identifies the "white captivity" of American evangelicalism. Rah, *Next Evangelicalism*.

2

PARENTS

Daniel D. Lee

In December of 2016, Jubilee Project created a five-part video series for "NBC Asian America Presents . . ." called "Jubilee Project: The Bridge," showing young Asian Americans connecting with their parents in a number of deeply moving ways.[1] Through hearing parents' migration stories, saying and receiving "I love you's," or having four minutes of silent, uninterrupted face-to-face time, Jubilee Project guides these grown-up children and their parents to bridge the intimidating cultural chasm and find the emotional connection. In the last two years, young Asian Americans created a number of popular videos that show the same sentiment of appreciation of and understanding for their parents, crossing cultural difference and generational disconnection.[2]

These videos' positive and appreciative view of Asian American parents help to balance some of the common negative stereotypes in our media. One of the most infamous Asian American parents on TV is Mrs. Kim from *Gilmore Girls*, which aired from 2000 to 2007. This Seventh-Day Adventist Korean American mother is obsessively strict and neurotically moral, while continually insisting that her daughter marry a Korean boy, who is preferably premed. Amy Chua's book gave language to the idea of

---

1. Jubilee Project, "The Bridge."

2. Lim, "Asian Parents React"; BuzzFeed Media, "Children of Asian Immigrants"; Wong Fu Productions, "What Asian Parents Don't Say."

the Tiger Mom and popularized this kind of narrow-minded Asian American parent.[3]

These overbearing Asian American parents have become somewhat of a trope in American pop culture. Of course, it is simply not true that all Asian American parents are overbearing. There are in real life some very understanding and even affectionate Asian American parents, as well as just your average run-of-the-mill ones. Nevertheless, the fact remains that many young Asian Americans have fraught relationships with their parents. This chapter seeks to break down the various aspects of this relationship so that it can be better understood and navigated.

PARENTS' VALUES AND CULTURAL HERITAGE

Children of all cultures are vulnerable to tension and conflict with their parents. Much of this can be explained through generational shifts. In their book, *Generations*, Neil Howe and William Strauss argue that every generation considers their values to be the norm, resulting in these generational conflicts.[4] However, along with these generational shifts, intercultural issues complicate the lives of Asian Americans. While some parents might believe that the problem is the younger generation's lack of knowledge of their heritage, the reality is always more complicated.

Asian heritage is more fluid and dynamic with "change, conflict, and contradiction" than what is embodied in the lives of the parent generation.[5] Thus, appreciating our Asian heritage does not necessarily mean acting or adopting our parents' views. Moreover, since all culture is fallen and totally tainted with sin, we would still have to discern what our faithful living looks like more reflectively. Theologically discerning culture is not about identifying what is good or bad based on some moralistic assessment.[6] For example, is the emphasis on the importance of education a good element or a destructive one? It all depends on what you are looking at. This cultural feature helps so many Asian Americans move up in life and achieve so

---

3. Chua, *Battle Hymn of the Tiger Mother*.

4. Howe and Strauss, *Generations*, 12.

5. Tanner, *Theories of Culture*, 53.

6. Niebuhr's *Christ and Culture*, a very influential work, described various approaches to engage culture. However, among its other problems, Niebuhr has a monolithic view of culture and also fails to adequately recognize sin in culture that must be judged by God, and not just transformed.

much. On the other hand, it also leads to inordinate amounts of stress and pressure to pursue academic accomplishments and cultivates a narrow view of success. Also, it does not help those who are, for example, artistically inclined. Or for a different example, when some non-Asian Americans and even Asian Americans elevate blind respect for elders as a cultural treasure, I wonder if they realize that this respect is intertwined with the hierarchical authoritarianism that many suffer under, whether at home or at church.

Critiquing and even rejecting aspects of Asian heritage does not make Asian Americans any less Asian. Asians in the motherlands are critically engaging their tradition so we can also be very critical of the tradition and still affirm our Asian heritage. In fact, these Asians are becoming cultural hybrids, negotiating their Asian heritage with Western values just like Asian Americans are, albeit from a different shore. Therefore, it is important to know that any tension with Asian American parents cannot be simply reduced down to a clash of Asian values versus American values. In sum, our cultural heritage is not the same thing as our parents' values. This critical distinction allows Asian Americans to accept and appreciate our cultural heritage as a part of who we are even if tensions exist with our parents.

For example, differentiating my understanding of my Asian heritage beyond what I had experienced with my parents has been an important part of my journey. In conflating my Korean heritage with my abusive father, I struggled to find much good in this part of myself. However, when I realized that in this confusion I had lost a part of myself, I began the long path to find and recover this Korean part of myself. The key in this recovery was realizing that Korean heritage was not limited to who my father was. Of course, over time I also came to see that my father's abuses did not define him either.

LOVE LANGUAGES AND WAYS OF DYSFUNCTION

Asian American parents' embodiment of Asian heritage is commonly expressed in their love languages. A different culture means that parents love us differently. In his widely popular book, *The 5 Love Languages*, Gary Chapman lists out five emotional love languages that we give and receive love: affirmation, quality time, gifts, service, and touch.[7] Chapman's focus is the marriage relationship, but he asserts the universality of these five love languages for all of us. Chapman's five love languages are ways in which

7. Chapman, *The 5 Love Languages*.

love is communicated directly, however, he ignores the more subtle indirect expressions of love. Russell Jeung takes issue with this limitation of only these five and proposes that, for the Chinese American context, sacrifice and food are also love languages.[8] Along with Chinese American parents, other Asian American parents express their love through sacrificing for the success of their children, often working long hours and moving to the best school distinct. They also express their love through food, often asking if we ate or if we are hungry. This, of course, is not to say that all Asian American parents only love indirectly. Some are multilingual and some might only speak one or two of the five that Chapman lists. However, if young Asian Americans limit the definition of love to what Chapman defines, they will fail to recognize the indirect affections of their parents as true love.

There are, of course, limits to these kinds of cultural explanations. There are indirect expressions of love and then there are relational dysfunctions. If there are different ways of loving, there also are different ways of abusing as well. The fact that there are unhealthy and even abusive Asian American parents is not surprising, of course. In *Toxic Parents*, Susan Forward give examples of parents whose negative pattern of behavior fill the lives of their children with toxicity.[9] Obviously, there are no cultural excuses for physical, verbal, or sexual abuse.

There are some more subtle indirect forms of toxic patterns that Asian American parents might possess. For example, because of the communal nature of our heritage, Asian American parents might be controlling to the point of not allowing the children to have their own separate identity. The child at this point becomes an extension of the parent, guided and controlled for the latter's purposes. The shadow side of parental sacrifice is that the children's success can be an assumed expectation. In this mind-set, having a trophy son or a daughter is an affirmation of parenthood and children's accomplishments are preconditions for parental affirmation of children's worth. Within this kind of relationship, it would be hard to separate what is really *for* the child and what is *for* the parents themselves even in their advice and guidance, because they are all *fused together*. If the children get an "Asian F," meaning anything less than an A, parents receive an F for their parenting as well. That is a lot of pressure for both parents and children.

This kind of abusive pattern hides well under the guise of cultural difference, but it is toxic nevertheless. For many young Asian Americans,

8. Jeung, *Home in Exile*, 175.

9. Forward, *Toxic Parents*.

being a "good" son or daughter feels like the existential core of their identity. Thus, they do not feel that they can admit to themselves that their parents are abusive or toxic if that is in fact the case. However, unless we can name these dysfunctions for what they are, there is no path toward healing and wholeness.

Abusive and toxic parenting exists. However, external societal forces continually influence young Asian Americans to take an overly critical view of their parents, to which we now turn.

ORIENTALISM, HONORARY WHITENESS, AND INDIVIDUALISM

What we have described so far is how the internal pressures of Asian cultural heritage act upon a child's relationship with their parents. What often remains in the dark in the minds of young Asian Americans are the external societal pressures of Orientalism and assimilation, which aggravate this relationship as well. Orientalism, which I mentioned in chapter 1, is a way in which the West portrays the East as the other, meaning abnormal, exotic, mythological, strange, and grotesque. In America, Orientalism is the way that Asian and Asian American bodies and experiences are filtered through a white normative consciousness. In popular culture, media, and societal ethos, this Orientalist perception informs a representation of Asian Americans heavy with negative stereotypes.

Additionally, Orientalism (along with Asian American racial phenotypes) serves as the ideological basis for the "perpetual foreigner" label often given to Asian Americans. Unlike European immigrants, Asian Americans are considered so fundamentally different that they will not be able to assimilate.[10] Of course, Asian American media representation has improved significantly in the last decade, with Asian American sitcom families and lead actors becoming more common, portraying more "normal" Asian Americans beyond the strictures of gross stereotypes.

However, the persisting and ubiquitous Orientalist representations impact the self-image of young Asian Americans as well as their view of their parents. Regarding self-image, Orientalist cultural forces, along with racist interactions and systems, push young Asian Americans to succumb to self-hatred and seek an honorary white status, to no longer value

10. Assimilation here means unhealthy assimilation into white culture at the expense of our Asianness.

themselves as Asian Americans. This pseudo-white status provides a way out of the perceived Asian strangeness in order to fit it, and the self-hatred is part of that package. In urban centers with large Asian American populations, the Orientalist pressures and racial oppression is often lower, but elsewhere the self-hatred can rise to destructive levels.

Whereas young Asian Americans might reject their Asianness to reimagine their identity as whiter, they also struggle with their parents, who represent their Asianness to them and to the world. As stated above, without other institutions and formative relationships that represent our Asianness to us, parents end up as the *de facto* embodiment of Asian heritage. Thus, all the Orientalist pressures exacerbate the child-parent relationship by making the parents seem exotic, mythological, strange, and grotesque. These societal forces are largely invisible and implicit, and therefore Asian culture and heritage are singled out as the sole culprit for intergenerational conflict.

Along with Orientalism and white assimilation, there are American values that are problematic as well. For example, the deeply American values of freedom and individual rights come with their shadow sides. More recently the postmodern turn in culture towards tradition, community, and narrative has rightly critiqued the shadow side of these closely guarded traditional American values. American freedom and individual rights cannot be read into the Bible to mean freedom in Christ or affirmation of individual worth. For example, Christian ethicists like Stanley Hauerwas have pointed out how many Americans cannot seem to distinguish biblical values from American ones, to the detriment of the church.[11] Within the home, these ideas about individual rights and freedom can misinterpret Asian values of collective awareness and interpersonal thoughtfulness as relational pathologies.

All of these societal forces work to caricature Asian American parents into stereotypes rather than multifaceted human beings. And so, although children generally come to realize how ordinarily human their parents are as they mature, the various external pressures complicate this process within Asian American families.

---

11. Hauerwas and Willimon, *Resident Aliens*.

PARENTS WITH THEIR OWN BURDENS

Because Asian American parents are usually perceived as authority figures, it is difficult to see them as just people, people struggling to make sense of their lives. Of course, all parents, regardless of ethnicity, race, and culture, have their own pains and struggles. First, all parents have to make sense of their relationship with their own parents. Just as young Asian Americans might feel distant and misunderstood by their parents, the parents' generation can have similar sentiments towards their own parents, whether they share about them or not. As stated above, there are basic generational shifts that are broadly applicable to everyone. To understand our parents who must investigate their own upbringing and past struggles, realizing that *"the single most important indicator of how [they] parent is how [they] were parented as [children]."*[12] Of course, any truth about our parents' upbringing does not excuse any limitations or shortcomings of theirs; but it can help us to understand them, and even be sympathetic. Along with their own parents, these parents are part of an extended family field, a whole web of interacting relationships.[13] Thus, the tensions and traumas of this larger system becomes a part of their lives and their parenting as well.

Immigrant parents also carry their own particular migration trauma and resulting loss, which might include "homeland, family, language, identity, property, status in the community," and more.[14] For example, coming to the US and being unfamiliar with the culture, language, and customs can lead to a loss of social status, which in turn can be channeled into seeking status, power, and recognition within their ethnic church or communal organization.[15] Within this scheme, becoming an elder at a church can feel like winning a lifetime achievement award. This same yearning can also be expressed within their family through the assertion of their parental control and authority.

The immigrant generation of parents experiences similar racial trauma and stress that comes from microaggressions and cultural Orientalism just as their children do. Along those lines, the experience of "the bamboo

---

12. Hendrix and Hunt, *Giving The Love*, 33.

13. Friedman, *Generation*.

14. Eng and Han, "A Dialogue on Racial Melancholia," 63.

15. Hurh and Kim, "Religious Participation."

ceiling" in their workplace could again lead to longing for status within their church or family.[16]

As I have gotten married and become a father myself, I have grown more empathetic toward my father. As I have stated above, I make and accept no excuses for any of his past abuses. However, confronted with my limitations and failures as a parent, despite all of my research, education, and efforts to be a good parent, I am filled with more compassion for him. I share this not to say that this will occur for everyone, but just to offer my experience of coming to terms with my father's humanity.

THE GOSPEL FOR THE FAMILY, PARENTS, AND CHILDREN

In thinking about the relationship with parents in the context of Christian discipleship, cultural values skew our reflections because parental authority is so entrenched in Asian heritage. In order to understand how Asian filial piety relates to the gospel, we must begin by remembering that gospel logic is death and resurrection, not mere tweaking and improving. Gospel works through radically changing what is meaningful, reasonable, and possible through this process of death and resurrection. Lesslie Newbigin describes gospel conversion as a radical paradigm shift in our frame of reference for reality, where our plausibility structure is transformed. According to him, anything short of this paradigm shift indicates that we are still in our old way of thinking, and thus still not fully converted.[17] Given this radical nature of the gospel, we must avoid at least two dangerous shortcuts.

The first shortcut is trying to make a direct connection while forgoing a radical conversion. For example, we could make a simple and direct connection between Asian filial piety and the fifth commandment of the Decalogue, that says, "Honor your father and mother" (Exod 20:12; Deut 5:16). While they may appear to be very similar, the radical difference is that in Asian filial piety there is no God to frame this honoring, and hence nothing to keep it from becoming an idol. However, in the Ten Commandments, the fifth commandment is firmly rooted in the prologue and the first commandment that says, "I am the Lord your God, who brought you out of Egypt, out of the land of slavery. You shall have no other gods before me." Moreover, while some theologians have tried to interpret Jesus as the filial

16. See Hyun, *Bamboo Ceiling*.

17. Newbigin, *Foolishness*, 64.

son *par excellence*, this can be problematic if the concept of filial piety is not radically reframed.[18] Otherwise, this move will only function to biblically legitimatize Asian cultural values, in other words, using God to serve Asian identity. This reading of our values *into* Scripture occurs often whenever we do not take the time to examine our cultural lenses. This simple and direct connection between Asian heritage and biblical texts ignores the radical discontinuity between the gospel and our culture.

The second shortcut, proof-texting, also avoids the needed conversion. Proof-texting is the strategy of using only a couple of decontextualized Bible verses to address complex issues. While all Scripture is God-breathed and for our edification, this way of engaging spiritual issues is problematic because it misses the grand gospel narrative of the Bible. For example, there might be biblical verses that "support" slavery but we know that those verses must be read in light of the whole witness of Scripture as it comes together in Jesus Christ. The same is true with texts addressing family matters. The Ten Commandments or the household codes in Colossians and Ephesians must first be theologically rooted in Christ, establishing the proper context for the family and individuals.

So, moving ahead with all these things in mind, we will see what the proper places are for parents and the family. While the family is affirmed in general, Christ decenters the family so that these most basic and important human relationships can no longer become idols. This is what Jesus proclaims when he says that he came to bring a sword between family members (Matt 10:34). Of course, he is not talking about abandoning our families, because later on he affirms the importance of our responsibility to our parents (Matt 15:5–7). However, there is no denying that, according to Jesus, our families simply cannot be the *most important* thing in our lives like in some Asian Americans' experience.

For our parents, their identity, worth, meaning, and security do not come from their role in the family, or from their children's success. Rather, their hope is in Christ. Of course, that does not mean that we should not love them, but we are not and cannot be their savior. The same goes for children as well. Our identity, worth, meaning, and security must not be rooted in our parents and family, but primarily in Christ. All this is so much easier said than done, of course. However, this truth is fundamental in properly ordering our family relationships.

18. See, for example, Phan, *Christianity*, 135–42.

Moreover, Jesus levels out all human authority and hierarchy by stating that in him we are all God's children. The theologian Karl Barth notes that, theologically speaking, there is really only one Father and we are all siblings.[19] While this is a radical and offensive thought to traditional Asian values, whatever authority we wield or submit to is relative to God's authority. We will see Paul making this very point in Ephesians below.

Focusing now more specifically on our parents, given this point about the gospel decentering the family, we can see what it means to obey our parents "in the Lord" as Paul says (Eph 6:1–4). Obeying our parents in the Lord means that we are acknowledging the gospel of grace as the basis and the framework for relating to our parents. Here are three reflections on what it means to honor our parents *in the Lord*.

First, we obey our parents while realizing that we are all sinners. They are broken and flawed just like us. This is a double-edged sword. Sometimes their demands are selfish and motivated by fear. This is true whether they are Christians or not, because they really are sinners in need of God's grace every single day. There is simply no way to whitewash our parents as always being right or even well-meaning, which would simply be poor theological anthropology. This recognition of sin means that cultural difference cannot be used to excuse genuine abuse or selfish parenting. Of course, we can always be rebellious, immature, and foolish in our ways. Practically speaking, what this means is that we need humility and compassion as well as honesty and truth in seeing ourselves and our parents. We might have to be repentant and be patient. We might really need to admit to ourselves that our parents are sinners in need of God's grace, just like us.

Second, obeying our parents in the Lord means that we obey not out of duty or obligation, but out of a free acceptance of God's gracious call to serve and to love. Martin Luther, in *The Freedom of a Christian*, said a "Christian is a perfectly free lord of all, subject to none. A Christian is a perfectly dutiful servant of all, subject to all."[20] Our freedom comes from the truth of the gospel that is the source of our identity and meaning. Asian heritage stresses duty and the fear of shame that arises when we fail to fulfill that duty. American culture is about freedom and individualism and the fear of losing yourself by submitting to outside authorities. However, the gospel casts out these fears with a God that saves us from them and empowers us to love and serve others, because we are no longer slaves.

19. Barth, *Dogmatics*, III/4, 245.

20. Luther, "The Freedom of a Christian" in *Luther's Works*, Volume 31, 344.

Christ frees us from the heavy burden of trying to be a good son or a daughter, because in Christ through faith God the Father says to us that we are his beloved sons and daughters, in whom he takes great delight (Mark 1:11). And because of this freedom, we can actually obey out of love and joy. God invites us to honor and love our parents, not because of who they are, whether good and wise or tyrannical and petty, but rather because of who God is and because we belong to God. Moreover, parents are to think of their role as a joyous calling instead of a burdensome duty. They can love and guide their children without thinking about the relationship as a mutually binding obligation of filial piety and parental sacrifice.

We should note that if we experienced abuse and toxicity from our parents, our love and honoring would look very different. In these cases, we might really need to look to our pastors, counselors, or therapists to guide us in wisdom. Our journey and process toward healing and restoration, or maybe mere survival for the time being, might be a very long and arduous one. We can see why honoring our parents *in the Lord* is so important. The same God that commands us to honor our parents will never turn a blind eye to oppression and injustice. God's commandments are just that: *God's*. They belong to God and they are an expression of God's love and care for us. They are not meant to be obeyed if doing so enables abuse or supports evil. Even the command to forgive needs to be properly understood in these situations.[21]

Lastly, with this freedom we can focus on obedience as a means to an end, as an expression of love and a path to connection. What we, and our parents, are seeking is real connection. Obedience should not be the goal because that's not what our parents, or we, deeply desire. Even though we might not obey our parents down to a tee, we can still look for ways to connect with them.

These truths do not necessarily make our lives easier. However, they are still the path to joy and freedom that God leads us to in the gospel. Like everything in life, it is only when we allow our relationship with our parents to die at the foot of the cross that we have freedom to enjoy it as God's good gift. Otherwise, it will be an oppressive idol, not only for us, but also for our parents.

---

21. Coulter argues that the command to forgive must be understood in the context of reconciliation and repentance. While revenge is not proper, forgiveness when there is not repentance is cheap and not justified. Coulter, *Repentance and Forgiveness*.

DISCUSSION QUESTIONS:

1. Meditate upon the truth that you are God's beloved child and God takes great delight in you. Since this love and delight come out of who God is, they never change. In fact, they *change us* to be more like God. What are some ways in which our parents give us insights into who God is? What are some others ways that our parents obscure who God is?

2. Reflect upon your parents as desperate and broken sinners in need of God's saving grace, like all of us, and fellow children of God. All this is true of your parents, whether they are faithfully committed pastors or abusive tyrants, whether they are found already, or lost and still sought by the Shepherd. Pray for them, for their lost dreams, for their past traumas, for their painful disappointments, and for their insecurities. How does knowing that your parents are just desperate and broken sinners like us help us to love and honor them in Christ?

3. Human frailty and brokenness impact us all. It can be difficult to see the relational dynamics with our parents clearly. Are there ways in which you have failed to honor your parents out of misunderstanding, hurt, or even selfishness? And are there legitimate concerns about your parents' actions and attitude that could have been abusive? You might need to consult others you respect, or even counselors or therapists, to help you discern. Ask God's Spirit to lead you to the truth.

3

FRIENDSHIP AND SOCIAL NETWORKS

Jeff Liou

The only soon-to-be-roommate I could get hold of before I left home for college, a non-Asian, told me that he really liked *Star Wars*. We made a connection. I was relieved. Our room was going to have four guys in it. I could never get a hold of roommate #2 (which would become a theme in his relationship to the rest of us). Roommate #3 was a wild card. He wasn't in the same program as the rest of us. He and I didn't share that many interests. Nevertheless, he became a very close friend—the only one with whom I still keep in regular contact. Perhaps, in a book like this, you can predict why. We were both Taiwanese Americans. We shared race and ethnicity in common, and it turned out that he had a group of friends from his high school that had likewise chosen to attend the same university. Suddenly, I was introduced to a network of Chinese, Taiwanese, and Korean Americans from the east coast. This became my friendship network.

I started noticing changes in myself. I soon found myself using the interjection, "yo," and other regionally distinctive speech all the time. Eventually, I began to eat Korean food just as frequently as I ate Chinese food. One evening, I came back from the store having bought a pair of cargo pants, and when I donned them for the first time my network of friends started playfully criticizing me by calling me "frat boy." I immediately felt an urge to dress differently.

38

This chapter is about social networks. By social networks, however, I don't just mean social networking sites (SNSs) like Facebook, Twitter, and Instagram. The broader topic of *friendship networks* is also in view. These days, we cannot talk about the one without talking about the other. Furthermore, Asian Americans experience social life and social networking in a distinct way that deserves explanation as well as theological reflection. This examination is intended to offer you some options for how you can engage the many influences that come through our various friendship and social networks. Let us begin by examining, first, the phenomenon itself and, second, what effect it has on us.

Designer Yang Liu has her own observation about this tendency and turned it into a wonderfully illuminating graphic in her book, *Ost Trifft West* (East Meets West). This graphic depicts the nature of social networks in her country of origin, China, versus those in her country of residence, Germany. People are represented by forty-nine individual dots arranged in a 7 x 7 square and connected, socially, by lines. On the blue, German side of the graphic, one notices just a few dots at a time that are connected by lines forming networks of two to six dots. On the red, Chinese side of the graphic, it seems that all the dots are connected together by a tangle of lines making the dots themselves less significant than the entire mass of connections.[1] One can easily observe what Liu has experienced. The proliferation of Asian American-specific Christian fellowships on college campuses since the 1980s is an important piece of evidence to add to Liu's experience.[2] I have heard others tell similar stories in their own words: it seems as though Asian American social networks exhibit a similarly high degree of connectedness and number of connections. In fact, this phenomenon is measurable.

Using data from social networking sites (SNSs) like Facebook, social scientists are examining the "racial homogeneity" of social networks and asking how such homogeneity arises. Researchers Andreas Wimmer and Kevin Lewis analyzed Facebook data from the 2009 freshman class at a small, private college and discovered that for this network of 1,640 students, racial homophily—the tendency that "birds of a feather flock together"—is one of several mechanisms through which homogeneity arises. Racial

1. Liu, *Ost Trifft West*. A preview of the book containing the image mentioned above can be found here: https://www.taschen.com/pages/en/catalogue/graphic_design/all/04623/facts.yang_liu_east_meets_west.htm

2. Rebecca Kim, *God's New Whiz Kids?*

homophily can be observed just about everywhere we go: our churches, our friendship groups. There are even differences in which SNSs are chosen by particular racial groups. Without thinking or trying too hard I found myself in a network of people like me.

The way that racial homophily works itself out is, however, actually somewhat complex. It is not as simple as saying that people from different racial groups only seek out others in their own racial group. To the contrary, Wimmer and Lewis pay special attention to Asian and Asian American students, concluding that, "much same-race preference is actually a consequence of same-ethnicity preference."[3] That is, Vietnamese students, for example, are more likely to be friends with other Vietnamese students, but not necessarily with an Asian American student of another ethnicity. If you have observed separate Chinese American, Hmong American, South Asian American, or Korean American Christian fellowships on your campus, for example, you may be witnessing the phenomenon described by Wimmer and Lewis. Similar things might be said about the success of Chinatowns across the country as well as their suburban counterparts where the concentration of Chinese Americans in high schools can exceed 60 percent.

Why is this important? The fact that we tend to enact homophilies of various kinds (by race, gender, socioeconomics status, clothing choice, lifestyle, etc.) is more than just a novel observation or factoid. The second force at work in my freshman year experience is called *diffusion*. Frequently, tastes and styles (e.g., what one wears, how one speaks, what one eats, etc.) diffuse across networks. That is, tastes and styles can be transmitted from one person to another, and on down the lines of the friendship network. This causes individuals within a particular social network to begin exhibiting sameness. There's no use kicking against the goads. Our friendship networks have a profound influence on who we are. Undoubtedly, this influence goes well beyond music styles and clothing to our identity and the choices we make down the road.

HOW MY FRIENDS LOVED ME INTO THE WRONG MAJOR

For example, when I was a high school senior in Tulsa, Oklahoma, I remember receiving a heartfelt gift from a dear friend of mine. It was a pen. A pen by itself might not have been so memorable. Instead, it was what was inscribed on the pen that I recall so meaningfully—"Dr. Jeff Ming Liou,

3. Wimmer and Lewis, "Beyond and Below Racial Homophily," 116.

M.D." As my final summer at home approached its end and we were all about to go our separate ways, I had collected a heart full of conversations with friends that all affirmed the same thing: I would one day be a medical professional as my father was before me and his father, a traditional, Taiwanese pharmacist before him. Even beyond that, my friends saw in me (as far as they could tell) a spiritual calling and the giftedness necessary to make an excellent physician. As I heard what I wanted to hear, my friends deeply shaped who I believed I was supposed to be.

Perhaps that is why I would not give up being premed despite the fact that my grades and my emotional health sank ever lower the longer I tried to "make it work." Spurred onward by the affirming story that my friends spoke into my life, I set out to fulfill all the academic requirements for medical school. I took the MCAT twice, I filled out the applications, and I very nearly hit "send." All these years later, I am embarrassed to admit that I lost track of that pen. Yet, despite having departed from the original plan, I still warmly and fondly remember my high school friends' affirming words that continue to shape me. My friends' hopes and well-wishes are still embedded in me as a part of my past.

This is both a testimony to the shaping power of friendship and a partial description of how a sense of self can be shaped. The "self" is not just simple passions or virtues. Neither is it the naked human capacity for reason. Instead, psychologist Kenneth Gergen has argued that because of the way we all live in a media-rich, diverse, and relational world, the self is now a "pastiche personality . . . a social chameleon, constantly borrowing bits and pieces of identity from whatever sources are available and constructing them as useful or desirable in a given situation."[4]

If it is true that the self is constructed by "borrowing bits and pieces," then the social network that surrounds us is crucial because it supplies the images, stories, norms, and arguments that become our inputs. If the network is diverse, the "bits and pieces" are diverse. If the network is not diverse, then the stories and possibilities that are spoken into a person's life might be more homogenous.[5] Both of these possibilities have strengths and weaknesses associated with them.

First, consider diverse "bits and pieces," or "fragments," as Gergen later calls them. They expand the range of ways in which one can imagine

---

4. Gergen, *The Saturated Self*, 150.

5. This is without a doubt a simplified description of how identity is affected by our social and cultural context. There is much more to say.

oneself. For example, when celebrities "reinvent" themselves, they dress differently, change their performances, find/leave romantic partners, etc. In the same way, Facebook affords us the opportunity to reinvent ourselves. Some people very much look forward to reinventing themselves and benefit from this opportunity.

However, when we see our friends' diverse and attractive lives through social media, many people feel the need to construct their own attractive narrative. This felt need to edit our public persona on social media is an escape from the messiness of real human relationships. Psychologist Sherry Turkle observes what many YouTube videos now parody: we opt, instead, for artificial relationships with our smartphones—some of us even sleep with our phones—which actually leaves people without real relationship and with a greater sense of loneliness. By her remark that "[l]oneliness is failed solitude," she means that feeling alone is now considered to be a problem that needs solving when, instead, solitude should be a regular habit cultivated even in children so that their identity formation process can progress as it should.[6]

Second, consider more homogenous "bits and pieces." A clear and consistent message about the self can create a deep sense of belonging and assurance that who we will become is congruent with our social network's perception of us. A sense of belonging can contribute to our well-being and our ability to resist incorporating harmful fragments. For example, the consistent messages we receive as a part of family life at home shape us so deeply that, for many of us, coming home feels like a warm blanket. Furthermore, the ability to carry this feeling of safety and security with us to college or into the work world helps many people to know that people at home have their back and that even their worst day isn't too much to bear.

However, there are also weaknesses in having homogenous inputs. Eli Pariser has cautioned us against what he calls "filter bubbles." The vast amount of data available to us on the Internet begs for "personalization" so that what ends up in our search results or news feed is really "relevant" to us. Pariser reveals that algorithms, or computer programs, generate the results, news items, and movie suggestions with which users are presented.[7] Hence, if one's social network is homogenous, or if one is consistent about clicking on similar kinds of friends, news items from diverse friends may stop making it to your feed. This became a constant topic on news networks

6. Turkle, *Alone Together*, 288.

7. Pariser, *The Filter Bubble*.

during the 2016 election season in the United States. Accusations of living in an "echo chamber" flew from one political end of the spectrum to the other.

To summarize, diverse connections and influences can fill our imaginations with possibility, but can also leave us feeling lonely without real conversation. Homogenous networks can provide a deep sense of belonging, but also become an impenetrable bubble. These "bits and pieces" are doing work upon our sense of self. In my case, God was calling me to a different career path, but God's repeated attempts to call out to me were muted by my homogenous filter bubble reinforced by my beloved and cozy network of wonderfully affirming, but homogenous, friends.

A TALE OF TWO SELVES: ASSERTIVE SELVES AND [NON]SELVES

Anyone can suffer from Turkle's "failed solitude" or Pariser's "filter bubbles." However, many minorities, including Asian Americans, experience even more profound effects of both diverse and homogenous inputs from SNSs. This is because many of us have been cut off from our immigration story, or we have not learned our own history in school curricula, or we have experienced racial trauma, marginalization, displacement, and so on. So when we find new and exciting fragments of identity, it can fill what feels like a hole in our self-understanding. For example, when one of my college professors put Fred Korematsu on speakerphone for our Asian American studies class and briefed us on the history of Chinese exclusion, I realized for the first time that I am part of an Asian American story that predates my family's arrival in the 1970s.[8]

However, in the social and political tumult of the last five years things have taken a disturbing turn. SNSs have lit up with strongly worded opinions, horrifying testimonies of racist mistreatment, and memes that use humor to poke fun at those on the other side of the political divide. These are *also* all potentially identity fragments that have diffused across densely populated Asian American social networks. They especially shape those

---

8. The late Fred Korematsu played an important part in Asian American history as a plaintiff in a 1944 Supreme Court case against the Japanese internment. He lost his case in a 6–3 ruling that has been effectively repudiated in modern American jurisprudence, though *not* formally overturned! His original conviction was voided after evidence emerged that the Court was influenced by false information advanced by the government.

Asian Americans who experience them in the same way that I experienced the phone call with Fred Korematsu. For better or worse, these fragments become a part of the way we understand ourselves and those around us. So, it seems important to me to highlight two outcomes I see among users of social media.

The first outcome is what I will call the construction of "assertive selves." Strongly worded sentiments and pointed stories on text-rich social media like blogs, Twitter, and Facebook frequently make demands of our loyalty while promising to constitute a truly meaningful self for new recruits. Their demands can be quite forceful and their calls for solidarity and uniformity of viewpoint can employ coercive force (rhetorical bullying, intimidation, ridicule, shaming, and even violence). In turn, the solidarity and uniformity they ask for must be asserted by the recruit. It can never be silent. In fact, "silence is violence," we are told. Strident voices draw innumerable lines in the sand and create friend/foe binaries even within Asian American friendship networks. This is a situation about which I am most concerned. As you engage with social media, you may come across rhetoric that is aimed at recruiting you *because* you are Asian American. Especially when this rhetoric is deployed *by* other Asian Americans, it can drip with guilt and shame, both direct and indirect. Such rhetorical tools are effective and can be devastating when they denigrate and disavow Asian American culture, origins, and dispositions. These voices make it seem like to deny their invitation, or to remain silent, is to forfeit your very soul. However, to accept their invitation does not always clothe the emperor. In the end, "bandwagoning" with the loudest voices of the most recent "trending" outrage isn't the only option you have.[9] Those voices aren't wrong to call out problems or call for action, but to do so by denigrating Asian American culture is beyond the pale.

When such loud voices dominate the blogosphere, it can seem like there is only one way forward. However, for perspective's sake, it's important to remember that there are many others for whom the self is an illusion to begin with. Hence, in the case of what I will call "[non]selves," there may be little restlessness or dissatisfaction to assuage. Many Western readers will have to take my word for it. Travelers and missionaries to different parts of the world, especially where Buddhism and Confucianism have

---

9. Those who use Twitter or follow online news outlets will recognize "trending" news stories as those which has been shared many times in a brief amount of time. Such news stories, as recognized by computer algorithms, will rocket to the top of the news pile, making them even *more* readily visible and therefore popular.

significant influence, might know this a little better. Loss of self can take the form of emotional detachment from the voices that demand to be heard and demand the hearer's allegiance. This self can't be bought because it has no economy. For example, to the [non]self, fashion either doesn't exist or it is a nuisance. It should be no surprise that this [non]self is unarticulated. Even writing about it despoils its pristine silence.

This detached silence is poorly understood, mistaken for complicity and frequently dismissed as lack of virtue, lack of assertive (read: Western) leadership, or insularity. Though, in the case of the last charge, nothing could be further from the truth. In fact, the potential for real solidarity might even find firm footing here. Rather than insularity, [non]selves, we now find, are good at adapting to new environments. Like water, [non] selves yield to shape of their containers, although as Chinese philosopher Laozi observes, the softness of water also possesses power to cut through the hardness of stone. Perhaps Asian American selves are so quick to be filled with fragments precisely because they are adaptable. Nevertheless, imagine my dismay when [non]selves are cowed into becoming assertive selves. Not all is lost. But something is.

In reality, many Asian Americans can exhibit features of *both* assertive and [non]selves. Many of my Asian American friends are finding their voices to engage the urgent problems of our day. The most thoughtful among these friends are finding ways to invite their social networks to ethical action and solidarity with the suffering. They assert a clear need for action while taking great (and often instinctive) care for the audiences they address. These same friends report to me the pressure they feel from many corners that they are both saying and doing too much, or too little. They struggle to decide which fragments to incorporate or reject. For me, it feels like being pulled between different poles, or different communities. Alas, it is difficult to find our way in the midst of this tension.

Asian Americans who are so deeply pained by and disappointed with their own Asian American communities of origin can sometimes disown them as they call for solidarity and community with diverse others. Sometimes hurtful rhetoric escapes through the fractures in and among Asian American friendship networks. Take, for example, elder Japanese Americans who have withheld information about their experiences of the internment from younger generations. It can be difficult to understand or express appreciation for those who endured unctuousness and silence in order to gain successive generations their voices. Disowning their dignified silence would be a tragic failure of the fabric of Asian American social networks and of the very relationality for which we all cry out. The fabric of our friendship and social networks is crucial to our own sense of self, so we must now reflect on it theologically.

UNITY AND DIVERSITY

The author of the Chronicles of Narnia, C. S. Lewis, known to his friends as "Jack," met regularly with a group of fellow authors. Together, they were called "The Inklings." For a time, they met regularly in a pub, The Eagle and Child, which still operates today. Lewis reflects on his friendship with J. R. R. (Ronald) Tolkien and Charles Williams. One day, their group changed when Williams passed away. Lewis says:

> In each of my friends there is something that only some other friend can fully bring out. By myself I am not large enough to call the whole man into activity; I want other lights than my own to show all his facets. Now that Charles is dead, I shall never again see Ronald's reaction to a specifically Charles joke. Far from having more of Ronald, having him "to myself" now that Charles is away, I have less of Ronald.[10]

In this quotation, you can see the way in which Lewis considers the fabric of his friendship network to be completely altered by the presence of each friend in the group. Lewis goes on to write that the more we share our unique experiences of God with one another by sharing life together, the more of God we will experience ourselves. Indeed, when we finally share God together with the great multitude of every nation, tribe, people, and language, what a sublime experience that will be![11]

To that end, Jesus began inviting diverse others into his family. What scandalized many of Jesus' detractors was his inclusion of outsiders. They are sometimes the "sinners and tax collectors," other times they are "Gentiles."[12] There was simply no room for these undesirables in, to bor-

---

10. Lewis, *The Four Loves*, 61.

11. Revelation 7:9 reads, "After this I looked, and there before me was a great multitude that no one could count, from every nation, tribe, people and language, standing before the throne and before the Lamb."

12. Lest we read the term *sinners* anachronistically, we should remember that it is just as much a term that denotes moral failure as it does social undesirability. Without a doubt, this was a social network of people, not just a moral judgment.

row Pariser's concept, highly filtered bubbles created by Jewish law and purity codes. The disciples were also scandalized. This is why, in Acts 15, the Council at Jerusalem had to grapple with the reality that Gentiles seemed to *also* be receiving the Holy Spirit. God's inclusion of the Gentiles was beyond the realm of the imaginations of those who had not seen it with their own eyes the way Paul and Barnabas had. Having received Paul and Barnabas's report about God's work among the Gentiles, those gathered in Jerusalem now had *new* information about the redemptive work of God in the world. So, it's not simply the case that Jesus came to gather as many warm bodies as possible. Rather, Jesus is the head of the *one* body whose members affect each other—we are to bear each other's pain, and share in one another's rejoicing. The body of Christ is more than just a metaphor for a social network. When we operate in the way the New Testament describes the family of God, we operate as a single, new organism, and we do so "in Christ."

Though many typically read "in Christ" as a vague sense of affiliation with Jesus, it is more likely that the phrase connotes a realm, sphere, or space in which we are to find ourselves—not unlike the "bosom of Abraham" from Luke 16. In that ample space, the members of the body are one *and* many. Unity and diversity are in perpetual motion, swirling endlessly so that neither takes priority over the other. In this space our oneness is not sameness. This is important for several reasons. Theologically, oneness is not sameness for the three persons of the Trinity, either. So, Christians should expect that Jesus' body is reflective of this affirmation of the doctrine of the Trinity that the Church has made through its history. Practically, the importance of maintaining both unity and diversity in the one body cannot be overstated. Jesus' inclusion of others, his intentional crossing over into Gentile territory, and his taboo-breaking association with the unclean all instruct the body of Christ. Campus fellowship, churches, and even individuals should carefully consider the ways in which social networks welcome diverse others, being wary of the many ways we can be unintentionally exclusionary. Devotionally, we are meant to be changed for the better by the delights God provides in the many-splendored body of Christ. Let me explain.

Remember C. S. Lewis' friend, Charles. Even though his passing might mean that he fades out of his friends' focus to some degree, he certainly continues to have a meaningful effect on his friends, often unconsciously. The

Dutch theologian Abraham Kuyper seemed to understand the "pastiche personality" that psychologists like Gergen describe when Kuyper wrote:

> Those people are mistaken, therefore, who imagine that the formation and development of our spirit and the formation of our person and our character are incidental, matters to which a child of God hardly need pay attention, because they don't matter for eternity. These do matter somewhat for eternity; *in fact, they matter a lot. Nothing is lost.* Everything that was essential profit here remains profit for eternity. And anyone who continues training himself until he dies, who continues enriching and developing himself, will one day awaken from being that richer child on earth as a richer adult in eternity.[13]

Not only can our friendships enrich us in this life, but these character-forming relationships and networks can change us for eternity! God is at work in our social networks, forming us. There is an unbroken chain of the work of the triune God within the creation. Pastiche personalities are a product of that work beyond any individual's machinations or reinventions.

In fact, passages like Acts 17:26–27 hint that one can rightly identify the handiwork of a God who lives in a diverse community. Luke records Paul's explanation of human diversity before the Areopagus, a group of people whose job it was to protect their community from strange and foreign ideas. The Areopagites were wary of foreign bits and pieces defiling their society. Paul introduced them to the God who created *all* of those bits and pieces. Paul explains:

> From one man he made all the nations, that they should inhabit the whole earth; and he marked out their appointed times in history and the boundaries of their lands. God did this so that they would seek him and perhaps reach out for him and find him, though he is not far from any one of us.

History, geography, culture, and peoplehood all "matter a lot." Paul tells these philosophers and decision-makers that these bits and pieces are arranged in such a way that humans would reach out for God, whose Son, our Lord, some of them would come to know by faith that day. To illustrate, my family history involves a journey from one country to another, from one culture to another, and culminates joyfully in *many* of my family members discovering the love of God in Christ Jesus here in the United States. The more I look, the more I can see God lovingly shepherding much of my

13. Kuyper, *Common Grace*, 568. Emphasis added.

extended family toward the diverse family that Jesus came to redeem. It lifts me to rejoice in God and in God's work for me and my biological family! God's work within the creation to raise up and expand this one family from every nation, tribe, people, and language really seems to put unity and diversity on grand display.

CONCLUSION

More than a nice analogy to which we might aspire, on the sixth day God created us like God—capable of real connection with one another. It just so happens that Asian Americans already tend to understand themselves more interdependently than independently. That is, living in two or more cultures simultaneously, Asian Americans describe their identities as filled with fragments of others. Additionally, having grown up interdependently, many Asian Americans display a habit of incorporating others' new fragments. This is where we must begin to think about responsible, intentional stewardship and cultivation of our friendship and social networks. Examining our influences can give us some clues as to how we are being shaped.

Sherry Turkle has been articulate about the failure of our smartphones and Facebook accounts to provide deep connection. I am not sure if it causes or is caused by the kinds of small and weak networks that Yang Liu depicted in her book. If Asian Americans thoughtfully steward highly connected, large networks, our habit of incorporating others can be a healthy transfusion in churches and communities that might benefit from it. If, however, we hoard what might be shared with the rest of Jesus' family, our treasures turn to dust. Similarly, if we despise the treasures from our cultures of origin, we are impoverished for it.

I will always carry with me my roommate's influence. Even though I lost that graduation pen, I have not lost my high school friends' loving concern. My network's ability to influence my tastes, my dress, my "likes," and even my career path is both a gift to cherish and a threat to manage. From Tulsa (1.1 percent Asian American in 1990) to LA County (where some of the cities are over 59 percent Asian American), and several percentages in cities along the way, I am working to hear from the Spirit of God to know who God is asking me to be influenced by today and where I can generate meaningful connection in the body of Christ. Here are some diagnostic questions to consider:[14]

14. While this isn't a scientific assessment, it may be a helpful set of questions to get

DISCUSSION QUESTIONS:

1. Who/what shows up most frequently in your newsfeed, and what do they tell about your friendship, social network, and lifestyle? (Tip: There are even apps and hacks that can show you the "personalization" process.)

2. Who is in your friendship or social network? Is it diverse or homogeneous? More importantly, what do you think of that?

3. How do you handle the "loud voices" on social media? If you find yourself shrinking away from them, why do you think that happens? If you find yourself outraged alongside them, why do you think that happens? Do you have an altogether different reaction? Explain.

4. Do you more frequently find contentment in new possibilities or familiar paths? Do you more frequently "like" your friends' exotic adventures, or friends' reminiscences? Why do you suppose this is the case?

you thinking about or feeling out some of your tendencies.

4

MONEY

Jeff Liou

A few years ago, I was strolling along Nanjing Road in Shanghai on my first trip to China, looking to buy some memories. On its own, this bustling shopping district is a sight I won't soon forget. The electricity, the colors, and the lights are evocative of Times Square in New York, only the neon signs are vertically oriented for the Chinese language. As I made my way to a certain part of the district, I was struck by a panorama of instantly recognizable marketing and branding . . . Gucci, Fendi, Prada, Burberry, Coach . . . and let's not forget 7-Eleven and KFC! I might have been able to write this off as an artifact of a city long ago populated by British and American settlers. But every city we visited that is designated by the Chinese government as a Special Economic Zone or Coastal Development Area exhibited this similar portfolio of foreign (i.e., Western) investment.

I had a strangely familiar feeling standing there, reflecting on what seemed to be the exaltation of Western enterprise. Where had I seen this before? It struck me: it's the same feeling I get when I drive through Los Angeles County's affluent cities that have significant Asian American populations. Cropping up in the midst of neighborhoods full of 1930s Spanish-style houses and modest ranches are new, enormous, European-styled McMansions complete with Italian granite, vaulted ceilings, and wrought-iron-fenced, semi-circular driveways. In those driveways, it's not uncommon to find a few luxury cars. (Though in China, it's not uncommon to find

American auto makers on *their* list of coveted import cars.) Yet, inside the homes, one might frequently find an entirely different collection of meaningful cultural symbols—a separate kimchi fridge, scroll art depicting otherworldly scenery or folkloric events, conspicuous inattention to coherent interior design. Strangely, this worlds-apart rift between the symbols that are on display and the symbols that far fewer people will see and experience are still somehow part of one, cohesive feeling.

It's also the feeling I get when I read Nielsen's publication entitled *Asian Americans: Culturally Diverse and Expanding Their Footprint.*[1] The report covers a wide range of Asian American consumer habits. According to Nielsen, Asian Americans are earlier adopters when it comes to electronic innovation, spend approximately 18 percent more than the general population per year, and are more likely to have a savings account. In 2016, the focus of the report was Asian American grocery store consumption patterns. However, in 2013, Nielsen described Asian Americans' spending habits with reference to brand names like Saks Fifth Avenue, Nordstrom, Neiman Marcus, and Marshalls.

Even though I grew up far away (geographically *and* culturally) from LA, I must confess: I, too, love a good sale on my favorite luxury brands. Perhaps this is why the feeling is so familiar—the habit of thrift passed down from the immigrant experience (and prior) converges with the habit of paying for quality. The ability to understand and anticipate these consumer habits make businesses better at luring in Asian and Asian American consumers. Let me say it this way: *You are a target being hunted.*

I can already hear the questions forming. "Are you going to say that there's something wrong with the house I grew up in? Did you expect my parents to build a pagoda? What's wrong with the multinational corporations and brands that I like making their way into emerging foreign markets? Can't we just trust the Asian Pacific American Advisory Council that helped put the Nielsen report together?" I'm glad you asked . . . but you're not the first. One college student once asked me, "Does the Bible forbid being rich?" We were gathered together, talking about the concept of "stewardship." The very moment that I answered, "no," I sensed an opportunity slip away. A room full of minds snapped shut, self-satisfied that the Bible is permissive enough to baptize our materialistic desires.

---

1. Nielsen, "Asian Americans: Culturally Diverse and Expanding Their Footprint." You may recognize The Nielsen Company as the agency which produces television ratings. They also report on consumer trends.

The commands in the Bible that *prohibit* economic exploitation and dishonest gain are clear enough. So, along with the rich youth of Matthew 19 we might be found prematurely blurting out, "All these I have kept from my youth!" Though I urgently hope exploitative and unsustainable practices continue to be exposed and are eliminated or replaced by responsible practices, the bar is still too low if all a consumer must do is *avoid* the "wrong" brands of chocolate, conflict diamonds, or polluting manufacturers. In this chapter, I will try to frame some values for things we should *do*, rather than simply focusing on things we should avoid. I will argue that Asian American Christian stewardship (including everything from personal finance to ecology) must carefully align our resources and consumer habits with the needs of our neighbors across the street and across the globe.

THE SACRED SAUCE

I will outline the kind of stewardship I have in mind momentarily, but we need to make a few more comments about the unique relationship between Asian American Christians and money. In this case, a specific matter deserves a specific treatment. It would be too simplistic to point the finger at ubiquitous, generic "consumerism." The phenomena of consumerism for Asian Americans need more careful narration. It's not just "conspicuous consumption" like owning designer handbags or driving luxury cars. Nor is it just "*in*conspicuous consumption" like obtaining an elite education or being able to participate in the latest health food trends. Both of these are frequently marked by the aspirations of individuals for either ostentation or for the humble brag. Rather, my concern is that consumerism among Asian American families can take a different form. Immigrant parents prioritize the economic future of their children and their children's children. At first glance, the financial success of generations of Asian American families seems like the product of virtue, cultural wisdom, or hard work. In fact, some onlookers decide that if Asian immigrant families can "make it" with this set of values, then other minority communities have no excuse. Additionally, Asian communities that don't bear the markers of having "made it" financially become ignored or deemed anomalous.[2]

2. This way of using minorities against other minorities is quite insidious. For those of us who have either been raised with or have attained the markers of financial ease, holding ourselves in contradistinction to other minority groups is a grave theological and ethical mistake. Hence, I think that there is much more than meets the eye when

Growing up in the eighties, my father, brother, and I would always scoop a spoonful of David Trần's "Rooster Sauce" into our *niú ròu miàn* (beef noodle soup). Trần's company, Huy Fong Foods, had just begun a few years earlier and this delicious sauce had already made its way from Rosemead, California to Cleveland, Oklahoma, into our home, and into our bellies/hearts. Trần's grandfather had moved from China to Vietnam where David Trần became a farmer, growing chili peppers. Years later, Trần and his family had no choice but to take the risk of boarding an overcrowded boat to escape the violence of the Vietnam War in 1979. To recap, we now enjoy iconic Sriracha sauce, a Thai-style sauce created by an ethnically Chinese man who left Vietnam and makes his product in Southern California. But the story doesn't end there.

Trần's success hasn't gone unnoticed and Trần also became a hunted target. As Huy Fong Foods looked to expand, the company was courted by the city of Irwindale, California. Soon after their new factory began operation, some residents filed a public nuisance lawsuit alleging that the odors from the factory during chili pepper harvest season were irritating their families' eyes, noses, and throats. Despite no violations of air quality regulations, Huy Fong Foods considered another move. Texas senator and former presidential candidate, Ted Cruz, tweeted, "#Sriracha may not be welcome in California, but you'd be welcomed with open arms and eager taste buds in Texas."[3] The potential job losses or gains and possible tax revenue motivate states to offer incentives to woo companies.

In the midst of it all, Trần's own position has been clear: "My American dream was never to become a billionaire."[4] Instead, Trần talks about making his sauce for those who enjoy it, plain and simple. Huy Fong Foods has never advertised Sriracha. He never patented his very simple recipe. The rooster logo makes it onto T-shirts because it's not even copyrighted. His son and daughter are president and vice president, respectively, of the company. Trần, like many immigrant parents, evinces an unassuming, endearing, self-sacrificing, and family-centered simplicity in the midst of his financial success.

---

it comes to the financial success stories of immigrant families like the one immediately following.

3. Shyong, "Sriracha Becomes a Hot Political Issue." As of the writing of this chapter, no decision to move has been made.

4. Shyong, "Sriracha Hot Sauce Purveyor Turns up the Heat."

I celebrate Trần's success. I even proudly wear a Sriracha T-shirt some-times! So, what am I worried about? Trần's story is held up as an example of an immigrant family succeeding in and contributing to the American economy. His story can all too easily be deemed exemplary and prescriptive for other Asian immigrants, and perhaps also for other minorities. If we are not careful, we can accept the standards of success that pit us against one another. Like water, we take the shape of the container in which we live. In fact, Chinese philosophers from Confucius to Lao Zi to Bruce Lee extol the virtue of being flexible, adaptive, and soft like water. While such *adaptability* is a great advantage in many situations, *assimilating* to these standards of success worries me. The line between adaptation and assimilation can be thin and the threat of losing one's sense of self (i.e., identity) looms therein.

Theologian Miroslav Volf reflects on this phenomenon in his book, *Exclusion and Embrace*. He wonders why it is so easy for people to lose their sense of self. In many cases, this leads to awful instances of individuals, having been carried along by a malicious wave, passively allowing them-selves to be sinned against in damaging and heinous ways. Instead of inde-pendently asserting a healthy identity, he writes: "It is not simply because [people] lack a sufficiently strong will to be themselves, but because one can satisfy the will to be oneself by surrendering to the other."[5] What does this all mean? Basically, one way for immigrants to "make it" here in the United States has always been to assimilate whatever outward symbols of success are in play—no matter the cost to the notion of "self." In his book, *Thinking Orientals*, Henry Yu tells the story of immigrants trying to "make it" in the United States during the period of Chinese Exclusion. He observes that clothing was an outward symbol of assimilation during a time when the way we now think about race and culture were being shaped (i.e., Robert Park's important "Survey of Race Relations" in the 1920s):

> Changes in the outer shell became tied to changes within, and clothing could measure the starting point (native dress) or ending point (American-style clothing) of such changes. When the body itself came to be seen as a uniform or a piece of clothing, then it, too, could mark the starting point for measurements of spiritual or cultural change.[6]

In other words, if Asian immigrants can become Christians and dress like Westerners, then *all* the different ways we identify ourselves, it was

5. Volf, *Exclusion and Embrace*, 96.

6. Yu, *Thinking Orientals*, 66.

thought, must be changeable. We can make ourselves whoever we want to be. Anyone can reinvent him or herself. All we have to do is change our affiliations and outward symbols—the things we consume.

Businesses feast on this particular feature of globalized free market economy, called neoliberalism, in which people and their particulars become commodified. After World War II, expanding markets adapted to the new conditions of global commerce. Economists, politicians, intellectuals, and the public, driven by a commitment to self-regulating markets, pursued global trade relationships that changed the global economic landscape. Political scientist Wendy Brown writes, "[Neoliberalism] formulates everything, everywhere, in terms of capital investment and appreciation, including and especially humans themselves."[7] The way Nielsen treats Asian American consumer psychology as part and parcel of business strategy is a manifestation of the way even human beings are viewed as capital. Political theologian William Cavanaugh takes a humorous *and* ominous jab at Taco Bell to explain how this phenomenon works in relation to cultural diversity:

> [J]ust as the food must be universalized and made bland enough to appeal potentially to the taste of *anyone anywhere*, to compete there must be a simultaneous emphasis on its unique qualities; advertised images must be rooted in a particular location, for example, the traditional Mexican culture of the *abuelita* before the clay oven, sipping *pulque* and shaping tortillas in the palm of her hand. Anyone who has stood at a Taco Bell counter and watched a surly white teenager inject burritos with a sour cream gun knows how absurd these images are, not just because Taco Bell does not conform to the Mexican reality, but because the *abuelita* herself is a manufactured image.[8]

Cavanaugh criticizes these market forces as purveyors of false "catholicity"—the illusion of fidelity to the local while actually supporting the uniformalization of global consumption. To put it in the least flattering terms, culture (including Asian American culture) gets warped into a commodity and when we participate in this buying and selling of falsehoods, one's own culture, marred beyond recognition, is sold back to the peoples from whom it was taken. The dangerous possibility of consuming lies about ourselves and others is all too real.

7. Brown, *Undoing the Demos,* 176.
8. Cavanaugh, *Theopolitical Imagination,* 109.

There are those, however, who are taking matters into their own hands and, in my opinion, changing the game. For example, the Fung Brothers are a comedy and musical duo on YouTube who understand their relative success as the assertion of fresh Asian American identity. YouTube is a kind of liminal space in contrast to Hollywood where Asian Americans have flourished culturally and financially. Using this medium, the Fung Brothers mix distinctive Asian American symbols and issues (e.g., food, parents, anti-Asian racism) with hip hop. For example, their video, *626, Young, Wild, and Free* is an exposition of their favorite eateries in the San Gabriel Valley set to the tune of Wiz Khalifa and Snoop Dogg's, *Young, Wild, Free*, which reached as high as the number seven spot on Billboard's Hot 100 in 2012. As of August 2018, their channel boasts 1.9 million subscribers. Content creators like the Fung brothers aren't simply consuming or parroting culture. It's not so easy to accuse them of being passively carried along by the waves of consumer culture. Just as it makes no sense to fault immigrant parents for wanting their children to flourish in a new land, neither ought we to accuse Asian American artists of "selling out" as they incorporate fragments around us in new ways. Having established that the waves of consumer culture can be resisted, we should now reflect theologically on a direction for that resistance.

CONSUMPTION FOR THE COMMON GOOD

No, this section is not just about making free trade, grass-fed, locally grown, sustainable, zero emission, and socially conscious purchases, as critical as these practices will be to our global future. But this section will share an important feature with the spirit of these practices: other-centeredness. If you consider the picture that I've attempted to paint in this chapter, you might notice that the consumption patterns are usually "us" focused where "us" equals family, or even Asian Americans more broadly. Many immigrants trying to "make it" are concerned that their families are set up to flourish for the long haul, not just the short term. Less thought is given to "outsiders." This creates a family-centered way of life that explains the enduring strength of Asian American racial and ethnic identities. It also helps to explain the relative lack of Asian American involvement in general philanthropy and global mission.

Though Korean global mission and recent developments in the burgeoning church in China are notable examples of what is possible, there seems to be much less talk of Asian *American* mission. It remains to be seen what the impressive percentages of Asian American delegates to the triennial Urbana Student Mission Conference will yield. No doubt, money and attitudes toward money present significant challenges to loosing the potential of the nearly $1 trillion of purchasing power that Asian Americans control for the sake of the common good. Currently, a lot of Asian American philanthropy and global mission are directed toward Asian diasporas or homelands. This is important work since many Asian Americans who experience material need are being overlooked because it is too often assumed that all Asian Americans are model minorities who have "made it" financially. Yet, by contrast, the authors of the Bible are so frequently focused on the welfare of the whole people of God. They are, after all, that people whom God has chosen, with whom God makes covenants, and for whom God sent God's only begotten Son. Focusing on the welfare of the entire body of Christ would be a great start for churches and Christians that would otherwise only send their ministry funds to their countries of origin.

Jesus' institution of the Last Supper broadens our concern for our diverse brothers and sisters around the world. Recall that William Cavanaugh criticizes consumer culture's lack of faithfulness to local culture by turning culture into commodities. His theological and ecclesial antidote to false catholicity is the Eucharist, which he believes "refracts space in such a way that one becomes more united to the whole the more tied one becomes to the local," and in this way, Cavanaugh, appealing to Galatians 3:28, believes the local assembly transcends its locality.[9] It is this transcendence that Cavanaugh hopes will bring the rest of God's family into view. I think this attempt is promising. However, I would add that Eucharistic adoration and liturgy around the globe and across the spectrum of Christian traditions *traverses* locality but does not necessarily transcend it. The diversity of liturgical practices around the Lord's Supper are evidence of irreducibly local influence on the practices themselves. Without denying the centrality of the sacrament, it is an oversight to simply gloss over these differences in order to center the ubiquity of the practice.

Instead of extracting transcendence from Galatians 3:28, perhaps the context of 1 Corinthians 12:12–26 is more illuminating. In Paul's corporeal metaphor, diversity is instrumental since "God has so arranged the body . . ." In fact, it's important to point out that Paul's teaching was meant to address a serious problem unfolding there at Corinth. The Lord's Supper was

9. Cavanaugh, *Theopolitical Imagination*, 115.

a scandal there. Some people arrived early and consumed so much that not enough was left for those who arrived after supplies had run out. In 1 Corinthians 11:20, Paul issues a harsh evaluation: "it is not the Lord's Supper you eat." This division fell along several fault lines that split the community. It appears that some in the church preferred Apollos's polished, educated speech to Paul's self-described lack of eloquence. A few had achieved new wealth while many were artisans or slaves. In a Corinthian house large enough to seat the whole dinner crowd there would likely have been upper and lower rooms that usually divided people by status. Paul's instruction in verse 33 is, "you should all eat together." In the next chapter, Paul expends many words to unfold the body's unity and diversity. God has placed these diverse people into the one body. Their divisions might threaten to undo their community, but this practice of the Lord's Supper binds them together, as Cavanaugh helpfully points out. So, to the degree that readers of Paul's letter to Corinth are to understand that God has divinely arranged the diverse parts of the body of Christ, perhaps Taco Bell (or Panda Express, if you like) isn't just an object of culinary scorn or condemnation. We may decry the "corporate" nature of chains like these, but I want to give us more credit. Most of us are aware enough and remarkably resistant to false catholicity to ensure that diversity brings increasing splendor to the body of Christ.

That last idea needs exploring: the diversity we bring to the body of Christ is a gift from God to be enjoyed and experienced by the people of God. The prophets of the Bible record cosmopolitan visions in which diverse nations and their rulers converge in one place to submit to the King of Kings. For example, if you take a look at Isaiah 60:4–7, you will notice this phrase, "the wealth (or riches) of the nations." Isaiah prophesies about a future in which the very best of every culture is brought as tribute to the enthroned and victorious God. In the New Testament, the book of Revelation incorporates these themes and even the language of Isaiah to talk about the final victory of God to establish a peaceful reign where "the wealth of the nations" are brought into the heavenly city whose gates don't need to be shut anymore, because God has subdued every enemy and there is no more danger of attack (see chapter 21).

We must be able to imagine, along with the authors of Scripture, that God's temple is decorated with the highest humanity has to offer, having made these things acceptable as offerings. These visions are an echo of Genesis 1, in which God says that creation is "good" and that humanity's stewardship and cultivation of the creation is "very good." To be clear, though, the God who owns the cattle on a thousand hills (a way of saying "everything," in Psalm 50:10) does not need human hands to amass wealth, as if such wealth would serve God. So, any earthly riches are to be understood in these passages as glad forfeitures of those who submit to a conquering King. Furthermore, God's cosmic rule over humanity and the diversity of human culture (not wealth or the accumulation thereof) is in focus in these passages. There before the throne, one might expect to marvel at the splendor and diversity of all the things that were once hoarded for human vaingloriousness, now placed under the feet of Jesus Christ.

To summarize, the Lord's Supper requires that we "eat together" with the timeless and borderless body of Christ, and God's cosmic rule over all of creation requires that human wealth adorns God's temple, not ours. The forces of consumer culture recognize neither of these priorities. We should not expect them to readily bow before God's throne. Asian American Christians must be wary of merely being carried along by the waves of consumerism that can only land us on the shores of a great discontent. The empty promise that we can "make it" by adopting outward symbols of success is unmasked as a lie.[10] More specific to the immigrant experience, displacement tends to make Asian American immigrant families focus inwardly on the survival of its members. The Lord's Supper and the Bible's cosmopolitan vision of God's great end-time victory inspires us to look outward, beyond ourselves. Such a vision, centered on God in Christ and God's coming reign, has more than the survival of one's own people in mind and requires a way of life to match that vision.

Cosmopolitan Christians are concerned about the welfare of others in an active way. Their checkbooks often reflect this. Because their treasure is in the body of Christ and the coming kingdom, their hearts beat for the good of all, not just the good of their own. In addition to charitable giving, when consumers are focused on the broader, or common good, they will funnel their resources and support into things that many people need instead of those things that they alone can enjoy. For example, when our oldest child was ready for school, we were happy to meet parents who had been investing their time, talent, and treasure in the public school system

10. See, for example, Lee, "Costly Signaling," 290–93. Yoon-Joo Lee's study examined the likelihood that Asian Americans' consumer behavior would be affected by advertisements that highlight a company's social responsibility. Tellingly, some Asian Americans were more likely to be persuaded by the advertising if the models in the advertisements were white rather than Asian.

for years before us. Maggie and Chris attend the church where I served for almost eight years. They were on the 2003 steering committee that birthed the Pasadena Educational Network (PEN), a nonprofit that encourages families to participate in the educational system that they are consuming. PEN partnered with some filmmakers who also attend our church and produced a documentary that gave an honest and inspiring depiction of students and families (many of whom attend our church) to would-be supporters and consumers of public education. We were persuaded to work alongside many other parents, teachers, and administrators to invest in a system that serves our city.

On the creator side, I am watching younger generations of Asian Americans catch a vision for using their incredible expertise (and purchasing power) for peoples around the world. Socially responsible entrepreneurship and Christian community development are changing the way business and ministry are done and the way we participate in our neighborhoods. I am happy to report that I now know of more than a few Asian American entrepreneurs doing other-centered work, and have had the privilege of watching some friends of mine make other-centered decisions about where they live. I met Jimmy Quach through a high school friend of mine. Jimmy started Good Paper, a for-profit business whose greeting card inventory is produced by God's precious children who escaped sex trafficking in the Philippines and young adults in Rwanda where disease has orphaned so many. Jimmy and a group of others live in an intentional Christian community where so much life is shared together.

I would be remiss, however, to pretend that all Asian Americans share the same level of freedom to make such life choices about their children's schooling or their career paths. The model minority myth makes many Asian Americans invisible. That's because the model minority myth is a rip current generated by exalting the symbols of and the ability for "making it" in America. If one is caught up in this current, it won't be long before the shore is too far away for us to be helpful. The alternative, I hope, is clear: *godly* other-centeredness makes us watchful for the needs of others (Asian American, or not) because God looks to redeem a people from every nation, tribe, people, and language.

DISCUSSION QUESTIONS:

1. Do you own outward symbols of success? If you follow the money, where do the profits go? Whose style are they most like, or is it something new?

2. If you go to an ethnic specific church, do they support missionaries? Where do those missionaries work?

3. What are the messages you received about the centrality of family? How does this benefit you? How might your family benefit others?

4. If you were to audit your consumption, what would it say about you? What expenditures express your commitment to others?

5

VOCATION

Janette H. Ok

"What do you want to be when you grow up?" is a question my teachers would often ask me. What do *I* want to be? That depended on another significant question: What do my parents—more specifically, my mother—want me to do? She had strong opinions on the matter. In grade school, I answered, "teacher." She modified, "How about professor?" In high school, I considered, "pastor." She recanted, "How about teacher?" In college, I chose to major in the un-lucrative study of religion. I remember that phone call when I shared this with my mom. Incredulous, she asked, "What are you going to do with that?" My plan: I wanted to be a pastor and a professor of New Testament. This would mean that I would go to seminary before pursuing my doctorate. Interestingly, and not coincidentally, right out of college I did become a high school English teacher and pastor before becoming a seminary professor. In other words, my various answers to the question, "What do you want to be when you grow up?" actually became a reality but at different yet overlapping stages in my life. My sense of calling from a young age was not limited to doing or being one thing.

Did my mother have a say in my vocational aspirations and journey? Yes. She definitely influenced my decisions, along with my faith community and cultural, social, and educational contexts. And yet my decisions were also my own and deeply personal. My sense of vocation was hard-fought and took time to discover and years to develop. In this chapter, when it comes to vocation, I hope to show that the creative tension between parental and personal desires can bring about a clearer, more resilient sense of God-given purpose.

The very question, "What do you want to be when you grow up?" sends the message that our vocation or calling is something singular, unchanging, and outcome-oriented.[1] But is it? Do we have one true calling in life and is it our quest to discover it? If so, then it's no wonder that many of us find the idea of vocation both so compelling and daunting!

The motivation to please our parents, honor their wishes, and make them proud strikes a deep chord in many Asian American Christians. The now classic but still relevant book *Following Jesus Without Dishonoring Your Parents* strongly resonated with me as a college student because I earnestly wanted to do both.[2] Apart from this book, however, almost every major Christian treatment that I have read on vocation pays little or no attention to the intergenerational conflicts related to vocational discernment and career choice for Asian Americans. Many books discuss how to discern one's vocation but do not offer the tools to work through family conflicts regarding career and vocation effectively and creatively.[3]

Asian American families experience a significant amount of intergenerational disagreement and tension over career decisions.[4] Asian cultures that emphasize group harmony and collectivism often consider what a person does for a living and with his/her life as a family matter. Western cultures that promote autonomy and individualism often consider career decision as a marker of self-concept, i.e., the way people see or think of themselves and feel about their ability, past experiences, and future possibilities.[5] Thus navigating competing cultural values and demands can be particularly stressful and difficult for younger Asian Americans, who not only see their career choices as representative of their personal passions, interests, or competencies, but who also hope to gain their parents'

---

1. I am very grateful to Elijah Sung, SueJeanne Koh, and Russell Jeung for reviewing this manuscript at various stages of its development.
Turpin, "Adolescence: Vocation in Performance, Passion, and Possibility," 85.

2. See especially the chapters by Jao, "Honor and Obey," and Cho Van Riesen, "Doctor or Lawyer?"

3. For a critique of some Christian books on vocation and calling and an alternative view from an Asian American Christian perspective, see Jeung, *At Home in Exile*, 177–86.

4. Ma et al., "Managing Family Conflict over Career Decisions.," 487–506.

5. Ma et al., "Managing Family Conflict over Career Decisions," 488.

approval and support.[6] In fact, conflict between parents and children is one of the most common issues raised by Asian American college students in counseling services.[7]

How then do we reconcile the individualistic "live your own life" and "make something of yourself" values with Christ's call to live for the sake of others and the "live for the honor of your family" values of many Asian immigrant families? I want to offer up a way to think about vocation (which I use interchangeably with "calling") in a manner that reflects its relational and contextual nature. Vocation fundamentally emerges from our relationship *with* and groundedness *in* the "One who *calls*."[8] However, our family, ethnicity, gender, and economic conditions also indelibly influence our sense of calling. Because calling is relational and contextual, it is subject to tension as we experience vocational conflict with God, ourselves, and our families. Not all tension is negative. Facing and negotiating conflicts in our discernment process may lead to a more creative and committed sense of who we are, what we do, and why we do it.

WHO GETS TO DECIDE WHAT WE DO WITH OUR LIVES?

Young Asian Americans have a tendency to react negatively to conflict with our parents over our vocational aspirations. We often idealize Western emphases on independence and self-determination over against Asian emphases on interdependence and parental obedience because autonomous career decision-making is such a prevailing American value. Contrary to white, middle-class Americans who are more likely to choose their own career path, Asian Americans are more likely to make compromises with their parents over career choice.[9] Sometimes it is assumed that parental involvement in the career decision making of Asian American college-aged children and young adults reflects a lack of maturity. However, Asian

---

6. Ma et al., "Managing Family Conflict over Career Decisions," 488.

7. Richard M. Lee et al., "Coping with Intergeneration Family Conflict," 389.

8. Brueggemann, "Covenanting as Human Vocation," 125. See also, Cahalan, "Introduction," 17.

9. Tang, "A Comparison of Asian American, Caucasian American, and Chinese College Students," 124–34.

Americans often include parents in their career decision-making process out of a strong sense of obligation[10] and familism.[11]

Moreover, our parents often see what we choose to do with our lives as an expression of our commitment to the collective good of the family, rather than an expression of our individual and personal passions and convictions.[12] They understand their migration to the US as the ultimate example of acting on behalf of the good of the family. Our parents' less individualistic and more communal and other-oriented paradigm sheds light on the conflict and tension many of us experience as we seek out our life calling within the dominant paradigm of American individualism. So how can we gain an understanding of vocation that does not lead to narcissistic individualism but that takes into account our passions, gifts, and the needs and well-being of others, including our family?

RECOVERING A THEOLOGICAL FRAMEWORK FOR VOCATION

Vocation is one of the most basic and yet elusive visions in our lives. We yearn for it even before we can even articulate what it is. So what is it?

First, let's begin with what vocation is not. Vocation is not necessarily the same as a job or occupation. A job is the work one does, usually to earn money. An occupation refers literally to that which occupies ones time or the principle work or activity a person does, especially as a means of earning a living. Vocation is also not necessarily the same thing as a career. A career refers to a commitment and investment (in time, dedication, and, I might add, school loans!) to progressive achievement in a particular field of work or occupation that provides opportunities for expansion and growth.[13] Our career trajectory may align with our sense of vocation, but we do not need to have a career to have a vocation. Rather, in order to have a vocation, we need to be called by someone to do something. As Christians, we believe the one who calls us is none other than Jesus Christ.[14]

---

10. Pew Research Center, "The Rise of Asian Americans"; Leong and Hardin, "Career Psychology of Asian Americans," 131–52; Ma et al., "Managing," 489.

11. See Jeung, "Second-Generation Chinese Americans."

12. Jeung, *At Home*, 184.

13. Loyd, *Your Vocational Credo*, 31.

14. See Keller and Leary Alsdorf, *Every Good Endeavor*, 2.

The term *vocation* comes from the Latin *vocare* and the Greek *kalein*, both of which mean "to call." We cannot have a call without being called by the Caller. For medieval Christians, vocation referred almost exclusively to the "call" to become a priest, nun, or monk. Later, Luther, Calvin, and other Protestant Reformers challenged the notion that only monastics and members of the clergy were "called" by God and sought to blur the lines between the sacred and secular.[15] They argued that God's holy presence was not limited to the celibate ministry of the priesthood and those in similar religious orders, but was also found in the work of the shoemaker, butcher, spouse, or parent. In short, they asserted that God calls all Christians (not just pastors, missionaries, and seminarians) to live faithfully as they work and to contribute to the well-being of others.

So what are we called to and how are we to relate to the God who calls us? Parker Palmer emphasizes the importance of listening when he writes, "Vocation does not mean a goal that I pursue. It means a calling that I hear. Before I can tell my life what I want to do with it, I must listen to my life telling me who I am. I must listen for the truths and values at the heart of my own identity."[16] Palmer reminds us that our calling is not the same as our own ambition or our parents' ambition for our lives. It is rooted in our sense of identity as God's unique creatures. There is something in our lives that is prior to or deeper than our cultural formation and socialization process. We do not will our vocation into existence, but rather we must listen to the voice of God who calls us into existence. We listen to this voice by listening to our lives—not our egos, which are self-serving and self-preserving, but our true selves: "Vocation does not come from a voice 'out there' calling me to become something I am not. It comes from a voice 'in here' calling me to be the person I was born to be, to fulfill the original selfhood given me at birth by God."[17] At the heart of vocation is the desire to be the person God created each of us to be.

---

15. It was Luther's belief that Christians, regardless of what they did for a living, participated in the ministry of Christ though their work. Because God valued all work equally and good works did not lead to salvation, Christians should also value work equally and not divide themselves into two classes—the secular and the religious. As Karlfried Froehlich explains, Luther not only made "vocation" accessible to all people, but also ironically "prepared the way for the total secularization of the term." "Luther on Vocation," 196, 199.

16. Palmer, *Let Your Life Speak*, 4–5.

17. Palmer, *Let Your Life Speak*, 10.

The danger, however, of framing vocation as a calling in which each individual has a true and unique task is that we can become anxious and self-absorbed in our quest for our special, one-of-a-kind calling and idealize our values as being in sync with God's values as attested in Scripture.[18] Vocation may lead to self-fulfillment and self-realization, but our individual self-expression alone is not vocation's purpose. To be called by God involves our sacrifice and response to what is needed[19] and a commitment to purposes beyond our own.[20]

Frederick Buechner famously explains,

> There are all different kinds of voices calling you to all different kinds of work, and the problem is to find out which is the voice of God rather than of Society, say, or the Super-ego, or Self-interest. By and large a good rule for finding out is this. The kind of work God usually calls you to is the kind of work (*a*) that you need most to do and (*b*) that the world most needs to have done . . . . The place God calls you to is the place where your deep gladness and the world's deep hunger meet.[21]

For Buechner, vocation involves the worshipful, joyful, meaningful, and life-giving work of inward and outward cultivation that leads to human flourishing. Such an explanation beautifully articulates the intersection of our deep need for personal fulfillment and the pressing needs of the world in the work we do. Yet the emphasis on what we "need most to do" and "a creative, significant work" suggests that we are already willing to do what God calls us to do.

In reality, however, the path towards fulfilling our vocation is often rocky and windy, and the work of vocation is inherently tension-filled. Walter Brueggemann offers the sobering truth that "We are always in tension with our vocation, wanting it another way or not at all . . . God's purposes for us and God's calling of us are in conflict with other ways we would rather live."[22]

While there is truth to the idea that we are more likely to love what we do when we do what we love,[23] we may need to love those we aren't

18. Jeung, *At Home*, 185.
19. Turpin, "Adolescence," 87.
20. Brueggemann, "Covenanting," 126.
21. Buechner, *Wishful Thinking*, 118–19.
22. Brueggemann, "Covenanting," 126.
23. Duckworth, *Grit*, 97.

inclined to love and do things we don't desire to do. Even if we struggle to see significance in some or much of the work we do, our vocation provides significance for all the work we do. Our vocation enables us to see any place as a creative space to cultivate grace. Jeremiah's prophetic exhortation to Jews in Babylonian exile reminds us that we are to work and pray for the prosperity and peace of those around us because in doing so we thrive: "But seek the welfare of the city where I have sent you into exile, and pray to the Lord on its behalf, for in its welfare you will find your welfare" (Jer 29:7).[24] Similarly, we learn in Proverbs 11:10 that "When the righteous prosper, the city rejoices." The "righteous" are those who willingly put the economic, social, and personal needs of the community (including their non-Jewish oppressors) ahead of their own.[25] Justice prevails when the righteous succeed in working for the common good.[26] Scripture calls us to care not only for our own well-being but for that of our communities, cities, and world. To work and pray for the flourishing of others is what God calls us to do even as second-, third-, or fourth-generation Asian American immigrants.

But let's be honest. We would rather live for ourselves or our families than for others. We would rather live for the "American dream" than God's dreams (or conflate the two as being one and the same). However, God promises his faithful covenant people the experience of shalom, not economic wealth and upward mobility. The Apostle Paul describes contentment, not wealth, as a sign of God's blessing (Phil 4:11–12). In fact wealth, according to Jesus, can be more of a danger than a blessing.[27] There is a strong temptation to buy into consumerist culture and to see the goal of our hard work as purchasing a stable and upward-moving middle-class identity.[28] For Asian Americans, the idea that we can purchase our belonging as an American is even stronger, since our parents gave up so much to become Americans.[29]

---

24. For Asian Americans Christians, pursuing the peace of the city can be difficult because we are often not included in the cultural or civic life of mainstream America (Jeung, *At Home*, 87) and are and are viewed as foreigners. See Huynh et al., "Perpetual Foreigners in One's Own Land."

25. See Keller, "A New Kind of Urban Christian."

26. The Christian idea of the "common good" comes from Jesus' commandment to love our neighbors, including the "least of these." Wallis, *The (Un)Common Good*, xii.

27. See, e.g., Luke 12:16–21; 18:24–25; Mark 8:36.

28. Jeung, *At Home*, 26–27.

29. Jeung, *At Home*, 27.

An Asian American emphasis on self-cultivation for the benefit or collective harmony of the community can serve as a corrective to individualistic self-determination.[30] Is parental input such a bad thing to consider when choosing a career path and discerning our vocation? Is a more individualist framework for vocation better? Rather than resent the fact that we come from family-centered and collectivistic-oriented cultures, we may do better to accept and embrace our contextual reality. And while we can understand the reasons why our parents may prioritize our socioeconomic prosperity, we must be careful not to equate our parents' or the dominant cultural ideas of success (Asian or Western alike) with God's vision for us. God does not cause us to prosper for our own sake, nor does God call us to seek the welfare of others only after we secure our own. To thrive, we must help others thrive. To love God with every fiber of our being and aspect of our lives is evident in the way we love our neighbors as ourselves (Luke 10:27). We speak, live, and act for the common good not only for the sake of our neighbors but also for our own sake because "to live just for ourselves is simply not the best way to be *human*."[31]

To work for the common good implies that we must find common ground among those who don't see eye-to-eye with us or share our sense of calling, including our parents! The story of how Gene Luen Yang became a graphic novelist offers us an inspiring and realistic example for how we can both pursue our more personal God-inspired dreams and find some common ground with our parents' dreams for us.

DRAWING DIFFERENT DREAMS: GENE LUEN YANG'S STORY

"Part of growing up is figuring out who we are, figuring out where we belong. I think there is a growing need and a growing voice for diverse stories in all of our media. As we as a nation grow more diverse, we want our stories to reflect that."[32] Here, Gene Luen Yang articulates his sense of vocation. Yang grew up drawing and listening to stories of his parents.[33] He loved telling stories through drawing and dreamed of becoming a comic book artist. He

30. On the relational basis of personhood in the Confucian tradition, see Hui, "Personhood and Bioethics," 34.

31. Wallis, *The (Un)Common Good*, 276.

32. MacArthur Foundation, "Gene Luen Yang: Graphic Novelist."

33. Kang, "Creating Stories with Gene Luen Yang."

butted heads with his dad, who wanted Yang to pursue a stable career that would make his immigrant sacrifices worthwhile and meet practical needs, such as a steady income and health insurance. Rather than reject his father's wishes, Yang and his father struck a deal when he went to college: as long as he majored in something "practical," his father would allow him to do what he wanted after graduating.

Yang majored in computer science. When he graduated, the comic book industry in American was teetering on bankruptcy and there was no demand for graphic novels. So Yang taught computer science at a high school for almost two decades, while creating comics as a serious hobby. It was not until his critically acclaimed graphic novel *American Born Chinese* debuted that he considered the possibility of making a living as a cartoonist. Even after enjoying success as a writer and artist, Yang continued teaching part-time for many years out of love for the job and his students, before reluctantly giving up his teaching position in order to dedicate himself full-time to comics.

Reflecting on his vocational choices, Yang learned how to find creative tension between pursuing his artistic dreams and addressing practical realities of adulthood. We do not have to know right away whether to pursue our dreams full-time. We also do not need to pursue our dream job in order to fulfill our call to serve others. We can test the waters and ease into our dreams. Yang recommends testing dreams in "adjacent spaces." As a teacher, he consistently drew and wrote comics and graphic novels at night and during summers. He published his early work at his own expense (which his day job made possible) and was disciplined about growing in his abilities as a graphic novelist and participating in the comic community, even while teaching.

What I most appreciate about Yang's story is how it offers us an example of how we might approach vocational and career conflict with our family during and beyond our college years. Yang made compromises, but they did not entail the loss of his own dreams and sense of purpose. Rather, his time as a teacher formed him, as evident in the fact that he describes himself as a cartoonist *and* teacher. Yang's story also demonstrates that passion and perseverance are not the same things. He had a passion for creating comics and persevered in developing that passion through practice, publication, and peer evaluation, while going to school and working as a teacher.

Just as importantly, Yang reminds us that our vocational discernment happens in community. Calling and purpose are closely related concepts because they are oriented toward others. Just as you cannot have a calling without being called by someone or something outside or yourself, you cannot have a sense of purpose without being others-oriented. Yang's passion for drawing comics, which emerged at a young age, matured over the years into a sense of purpose to create stories that reflect the growing diversity of our nation. His ability to draw comics for a living did not come about until after he learned to develop his passions in adjacent vocational spaces that were shaped with others.

IN SEARCH OF VOCATIONAL SPACES

A recent study found that when Asian immigrant children are willing to empathize with their parents' concerns and develop strategies to balance personal happiness and familial obligation, they were able to pursue their own goals with some adjustment based on parental input.[34] The most effective strategy for obtaining parental approval was by educating parents about their career choice, e.g., explaining the viability of their career through conversations, inviting parents to work-related events, or seeking support from outside sources, such as a trusted relative or respected figure in the community with knowledge of that career.[35]

The study concluded that it is possible for Asian American younger adults to find a "middle ground" and make certain compromises without giving up their own desired careers.[36] We might begin searching for this middle ground by working in the field that our parents approve of for several years before pursuing our personal passions, or by creatively inserting the time to explore and develop our interests within or adjacent to a practical career before deciding to go "full-time" in what we sense God is calling us to do. Younger adulthood is especially a stage in which we learn to hold our multiple callings in creative tension, working out with trial and error the balance between work and relational life while engaging in the hard work of self-discovery.[37]

---

34. Ma et al., "Managing," 498.
35. Ma et al., "Managing," 499–500.
36. Ma et al., "Managing," 501.
37. Turpin, "Younger Adulthood," 97–98.

Another way to help our parents be more open to our "dream job" is by showing that we are competent and committed to reaching our goals. Our parents may not agree with or share our enthusiasm for what God is calling us to do. They may, however, be able to take our calling more seriously when they see that we are not only excited about God's callings for us, but that we also have the endurance and grit to do it even when our enthusiasm wanes. Passion, as Angela Duckworth explains, is not reflected in how strongly you feel about something but in "how *steadily* you hold to goals over time."[38] Does our devotion to God and God's calling for our lives endure? Do the ways we prioritize our lives reflect our sense of calling, kingdom values, and career goals? Our parents may highly value job security. But if they see how we are able to be financially responsible and independent[39] while also showing generosity to them and others, they may at least concede that we are good stewards of our money and can make ends meet. Also, if we honor our parents in non-financial ways, such as taking the time to visit or call them or helping them with their tech questions or housework, they may take us more seriously because they see us thinking beyond ourselves and acting more like caring and responsible adults. Part of living a mature and integrated vocational life is learning how to live into multiple and simultaneous callings *while* including our parents in the process.

CONCLUSION

Rather than think of vocation as landing that dream job or pursuing the career we love, Scripture helps us imagine vocation as living more faithfully according to the dreams of the God who calls us and grounds our being.[40]

What does God dream for the world? Many things! But for starters, God dreams that we demonstrate our love for him through the way we love our neighbors (Matt 22:35–40). God dreams that we live and work to

---

38. Duckworth, *Grit*, 58.

39. By financially "independent" I do not mean to say that living on your own is superior to living under a multi-generation roof and having a shared family income. Many Asian Americans help financially support their aging parents and have them live in their own homes and vice-versa. But many Asian American younger people also live in their parents homes indefinitely and benefit from their financial support even while working, which makes it difficult to prove to their doubtful parents that they know and have what it takes to survive.

40. Brueggemann, "Covenanting," 126.

cultivate peace, security, justice, and prosperity for those in our communities, congregations, schools, places of work, and neighborhoods (Jer 29:7), and those far beyond our cities (Acts 1:8). God dreams that we be "the *best possible* citizens of [our] earthly cities"[41] and by doing so offer others a foretaste of the coming kingdom.[42] Working for the common good or for "the goal of justice," as Martin Luther King reminds us, "requires sacrifice, suffering, and struggle; the tireless exertions and passionate concern of dedicated individuals"[43] and, I must add, dedicated members of the church. Russell Jeung rightly emphasizes, "Our calling is not an individual one; it is a collective one to be God's new people."[44] Our primary vocation is to be the church for others.

Your particular callings are for you to discover, but you can't go it alone! The body of Christ plays a vital role in discerning your unique calling in Christ because as Christians, we are called into the community of the church before we are called into the world (the Greek word, *ekklesia*, translated as "church" actually contains the verb "to call").[45] This does not mean, however, that the gifts God gives us to edify the body of Christ cannot be used outside of the church to serve the common good. The process of discerning how we will be a part of what God is doing in the world takes time, and we need the guidance of the Holy Spirit and the wisdom of others, including our parents, to help us. That said, figuring out what God is calling you to do is a lot less elusive than you think: God calls you "to do justice, to love kindness, and to walk humbly with our God" (Mic 6:8). When you participate in the renewal of the communities around you, including your own families, you will find vocational spaces everywhere you go.

DISCUSSION QUESTIONS:

1. What did you enjoy doing over and over again when you were younger? What activities, no matter how challenging, give you life as you do them? What dreams did you have for yourself when you were little? What do you dream of doing with your life now and why?

41. Keller, "A New Kind of Urban Christian."
42. Sherman, *Kingdom Calling*, 27.
43. King, "Address at the Thirty-fourth Annual Convention."
44. Jeung, *At Home*, 191.
45. Cahalan, "Callings," 17.

2. What parental and internal conflicts have you faced regarding your dreams, values, and career aspirations? What kind of conversations might you have with your parents regarding your sense of calling (even if they're not Christians) and career choice? What middle or common ground might you find with your parents over what you want to do with your life? How might the idea of searching for vocation in adjacent spaces manifest itself while you're in college, grad school, or working?

3. In what ways do you think God's justice and care for those in need shapes what you want to do with your life and how you want to do it?

6

RACIAL IDENTITY

Hak Joon Lee

Jeremy Lin, a Taiwanese American, was the Cinderella story of the 2011–2012 NBA season. Though previously mostly unknown to the public, he shocked the world with his sensational performance as a New York Knicks point guard. During the season, he led the Knicks on a startling winning streak, beating Kobe Bryant's LA Lakers. Jeremy Lin's No. 17 jersey instantly became the NBA's top seller; furthermore, his merchandise was shipped to twenty-three different countries, contributing to the soaring rise in his team's stock price. His fame raked in $170 million for the Knicks.

Among the millions of fans here in the US and overseas who cheered for Jeremy Lin, Asian Americans were especially ecstatic. They went into a frenzy; even those who had rarely watched professional basketball began to view his games, and many constantly followed his news clips. Many showed up at his games, waving, shouting, and dancing. They were at the center of a phenomenon called *Linsanity*.

Why were so many Asian Americans exhilarated by Jeremy Lin? What is the source of Linsanity among Asian Americans?

There are several forces driving Linsanity among Asian Americans. Jeremy is the first major Asian American star player in the NBA, and his breakthrough helped challenge several stereotypes about Asian Americans—that they are passive, awkward, naïve, nerdy, and boring; that they are not sexy, nor masculine; and that overall they are just not very cool.

Jeremy countered the stereotypes and proved that Asian American could be athletic, smart, masculine, sophisticated, and, yes, sexy and cool. He symbolizes the best of Asian and American hybridity—he is superbly academic and athletic, a Harvard graduate and a star NBA player. Where can one find a better combination?

Beyond basketball, the phenomenon of Linsanity among Asian Americans has to do with the issue of their identity. He boosted the self-respect and pride of many Asian Americans. Young Asian Americans found in Jeremy not only a sports star, but also a good role model with whom they could positively identify in their struggles against social stereotypes. In addition, for many evangelical Asian Americans, he has a special appeal because he is one of them.

Jeremy is writing a new script for Asian Americans, supplanting a part of the old social script of many in US society.

Barely noticed in the mainstream media, but equally important, is that Jeremy's parents also broke stereotypes for Asian immigrants. They supported Jeremy's passion for basketball even as they pushed him toward academic excellence. Although they were criticized by their friends for allowing Lin to play so much basketball, they let him pursue his passion. Asian Americans see in his parents a new model of Asian parents who are not overly strict "tiger moms"[1] or dads, but are sensitive to the passions of their children.

ASIAN AMERICAN RACIAL IDENTITY

Young Asian Americans' wild enthusiasm about Jeremy's success highlights an often overlooked part of their lives: their racial identity. Racial identity is a specific dimension of one's identity defined by membership in a particular racial group. That is, it is a person's sense of self that arises as he/she belongs to a certain racial group. Racial identity is not inherent, but is socially constructed. Nevertheless, it has an ascriptive, regulatory power over individuals because of the highly racialized nature of social relationships and cultural mores in the West. Racialization has happened through a long-standing history of Western colonialism and political hegemony, which have exploited science and philosophy to systematically categorize humans into different racial groups on the pseudo-scientific basis of physical traits.

---

1. Chua, *Battle Hymn of the Tiger Mother*.

In a racialized society, the issue of identity cannot be discussed apart from racial identity; racial identity constitutes an integral part of selfhood.

Here is a brief explanation of how racial identity is associated with identity development (or underdevelopment), and how it affects one's sense of self-worth:

Our sense of self (identity) initially emerges through other people's perception of us. A famous social psychologist, Charles Horton Cooley, called it the "looking glass self." That is, significant people in our lives function like a mirror that constantly reflects our images back to us. These significant others could be our parents, grandparents, close friends, teachers, and/or prevalent cultural images, depending on who our reference group is. As social animals, we take and internalize these images reflected to us by the "mirrors" of others. However, "a social mirror" is different from an ordinary mirror; it reflects back to us through people's own perceptions and interpretations of our appearances and behaviors, which could be positive or negative, correct or distorted.

Identity formation takes place smoothly when one's perception of the self and others' perceptions (mirrored images) are congruent, and when images are mostly affirming and positive. However, enduring consistently incongruent or negative images causes problems in the self. A person faces a difficult choice about what to do with the refracted images, especially when images are sent back by significant others. A dilemma also arises when the negative mirroring focuses on aspects of the self that are inborn: gender, race, physical traits, etc. For example, in a patriarchal society, a woman faces difficulty in developing a healthy identity as society constantly portrays women as emotional, irrational, and therefore poor leaders.

Approaching the issue from a more macro angle, culture serves as a mirror for identity formation. A significant force of formation, culture is a scripted system of values, preferences, and biases that are supported by tradition and social mores. It defines and communicates what is good or bad, beautiful or ugly, acceptable or unacceptable, favorable or unfavorable. Cultural scripts operate beyond individuals' control, though they are not entirely unchangeable. A stereotype, a form of social script, is the particular way that a society, and usually a majority group within that society, imposes a script upon a minority group. A stereotype negatively affects self-esteem, instilling a sense of inferiority in the members of a minority group. These damaging scripts function as powerful "identity mirrors" for individuals, guiding and regulating their choices and actions.

The issue of racial identity poses a particular challenge for Asian Americans due to their social position between two starkly different cultures. As with other racial minority groups, various negative images of Asian Americans are extensively reflected in mass media and popular culture. Asian Americans unconsciously internalize these images as they try to fit into the dominant culture under various pressures to survive and succeed. However, unlike African Americans and Latin Americans, the racial identity of Asian Americans has a unique dimension due to the entrenched social stereotype of perpetual foreigners, their distinctive Asian cultural heritage and traditions, their strong ties with their families, and excessive pressure for academic achievement and professional success. The following section briefly examines two primary forces that affect the identity formation of young Asian Americans: family and society.

FRACTURED MORAL UNIVERSES
AND SOCIAL PRESSURES

Family

For every human being, the family is the most important institution for identity development. A person is born into and grows in a family of some kind. Identity first develops through a person's interaction with the members of the family (parents, siblings, and relatives). However, the family also exists in a particular culture, and that cultural tradition inevitably affects individuals. In other words, culture is the deposit or reservoir of a particular way of understanding reality (deity, humans, and the world), and such understanding is shared and passed down through social customs, mores, and practices in various social institutions, including (and especially!) the family.

Although many Asian immigrants have adopted a Western lifestyle and so many are increasingly open-minded, a traditional communal culture is nevertheless still very much alive among many families. Compared to white parents, Asian immigrants tend to be more communal, patriarchal, and family-oriented. Many parents are willing to sacrifice for the sake of their children, but the downside is that individual idiosyncrasy, assertiveness, and personal boundaries are not well respected at home. Traditionally, a child's identity is coterminous with the identity of the family or clan. Children are typically instructed that their primary duty is to respect and obey their parents' wishes, which include decisions about their education, love life, and occupation. Although this relational dynamic is changing as more Asian immigrant parents are exposed to individualistic Western cultural norms, it is still influential among Asian immigrants, and even among second-generation Asian Americans, as one sees in the "Tiger Mom" story. For some Asian immigrants, personal identity is still very much bound up with one's family. Children are expected to enhance, or at least not harm, the family's honor and reputation through their academic and economic success.[2] The honor of one's family is decided by wealth, academic prestige, profession, and family lineage. The criterion of performance or success is usually very narrowly quantified by certain achievements: standardized test scores, school rankings, annual salaries, etc. Parents from East Asia with a strong Confucian culture tend to deeply care about their children's education. In fact, many of them immigrate to the US, or decide to stay after their initial visits, for better opportunities for their children.

Unfortunately, this parental pressure for educational success is reinforced in a global society where high un- or under-employment among young people of all ethnicities is growing. The increasing number of YouTube videos that ridicule the obsession of Asian immigrant parents with academic success discloses the level of mental stress that young people experience in their families. Parents' focus on achievement and perfectionism often leads to little tolerance for the mistakes and academic failures of their children.

Many Asian American young people live under constant pressure to achieve academic and professional success, often with only limited career choices. For those Asian American young adults whose immigrant parents are economically struggling, there is an extra burden, usually resulting in feelings of guilt or inadequacy, to perform well at school or work, as they feel morally obligated to compensate for their parents' personal sacrifices for them. This sense of guilt has worsened in recent years, as more Asian American young people live with their parents until they find jobs.

Furthermore, although living in geographically segregated racial-ethnic enclaves ("Koreatown," Chinatown," "Little Tokyo," etc.) helps Asian immigrants emphasize the importance of their ethnic heritages and traditions as a way of reinforcing dignity and self-esteem, it can also heighten young Asian Americans' struggle with identity. Immigrant parents frequently

2. Kodama et al., "An Asian American Perspective on Psychological Student Development Theory," 54.

teach their mother tongues, maintain traditional customs, and insist their children find spouses within the same ethnic groups, but fail to carefully attend to the complex history of race and race relationships in the US and their complicated influences on the identity development of their children. They often believe that academic success and fluency in English will resolve all the tensions faced by their children. Young Asian Americans experience difficulty in developing a healthy sense of racial identity because racial identity, compared to other dimensions of identity such as gender roles, social status, etc., is seldom discussed in the Asian immigrant community.

Racialized Society

Although the family is the primary institution of identity formation, schools and mass media are also major forces that contribute to the shaping of identity, especially in this information age. Like family, schools and mass media are not culturally neutral. They circulate and promote a particular worldview and value system—a way of understanding reality, including race and ethnicity. Despite the great progress it has made, the US is still a highly racialized society. From former President Obama to a new immigrant from China, race is an issue that any person of color cannot escape. Race is a primary identity marker in society; it is the first social category with which people identify others. Racial stereotypes are still very much alive in many parts of the nation. From its beginning, the US was built upon a racial caste system. People of color have been continuously subjected to racial discrimination in the US, as attested by the nation's history of colonial conquest, slavery, segregation, and other abuses. Asian Americans have been no exception. The Chinese Exclusion Act, the exploitation of Chinese laborers, the hysteria of "yellow peril," the Japanese Internment, and the LA Riots are only a few examples of discrimination against Asian Americans.[3] Whether they were born here or not, no matter how long they have lived in the US, no matter how fluently they speak English, Asian Americans still cannot completely free themselves from negative stereotypes. White privilege and power are still hidden in various aspects of American society despite its proud claims of diversity and inclusiveness. Even today, Asian Americans are often treated as perpetual foreigners, not as genuine members of society. They are treated as if they do not belong here.

---

3. Chapter 9 discusses this aspect in further detail.

It is often the case with their college life as well. For example, psychological and emotional needs of Asian Americans are not adequately recognized and addressed in many colleges. Professional college counselors for Asian Americans are underrepresented. Asian Americans are expected to take care of themselves because they are typically considered to be the model minority (a back-handed compliment) or because college administrators and staff do not care enough about them due to a hidden bias against Asian Americans as perpetual foreigners. Their history and their stories are missing in college curricula. The question of race is still primarily framed in society as black vs. white. On the other hand, the model minority myth has the effect of isolating Asian Americans from other racial groups as it creates unnecessary competition and comparison. While white people are threatened by Asian Americans' academic and vocational success, other people of color are threatened by Asian Americans' closer proximity to whiteness and privilege. From either perspective, Asian Americans are left on the outside.

CAUGHT BETWEEN TWO DIFFERENT MORAL UNIVERSES

Asian Americans struggle with a gap between the dominant social script of white culture (which tends to be negative and demeaning toward them) and the traditional Asian cultural script of their parents (which tends to be tribalistic yet indifferent toward issues of race and racial identity).

They are pulled by the values of individual freedom, self-actualization, and creativity on the one hand, and the values of community, family, duty, and obligations to parents on the other. Being caught between the two different universes causes many, perhaps ironically, to feel inadequate in both—they are not fully Asian by their parents' or church members' standards due to linguistic and cultural barriers, and not fully American by their white peers' standards due to racism and cultural isolation. Asian Americans struggle as they carry both the burden of parental expectations and the burden of mainstream social pressures.

Furthermore, there is no established frame of reference for Asian Americans that defines cultural expectations and boundaries. The scarcity of good role models, mentors, or support groups for Asian American youths means that healthy identity development often remains an individual struggle rather than being embraced as a communal responsibility.

Many run to friends because they seem to be the only comfortable group to hang around. The split nature of their moral universe and the lack of proper family or community support hinders young Asian Americans from developing a coherent sense of identity. And yet they are aware that the stakes are terribly high: if the balancing act between cultural differences is not smoothly negotiated it can result in alienation from their parents or ostracism from society. The high suicide and depression rate among Asian American youth reveals the depth of alienation and confusion that they are experiencing.

Trapped between two contrasting worlds, there is a temptation to choose one culture over the other because of the human tendency to seek coherence in one's moral universe. There is a strong urge among Asian Americans either to assimilate to the dominant culture by disidentifying themselves from Asian culture, or to remain within the boundary of their ethnic communities by hanging around friends of the same ethnicity, mostly listening to Asian songs, eating Asian food, or taking care of parents' small businesses in Asian towns.

However, neither cultural assimilation nor ethnic isolation solves the problem. Assimilation may ease internal cultural tension, but it is unable to challenge the ongoing racism in the US. Likewise, isolation may help temporarily avoid certain challenges, but it cannot meaningfully address them, as Asian Americans will thus be excluded from public debates and important social decisions. However, Asian Americans do not have to choose one culture over the other—both are equally important. While the family and ethnic community are the places of their emotional attachment and belonging, schools and society are the places of their learning, professional life, and civic responsibility.

Asian Americans need to develop a balanced sense of racial identity in order to peacefully navigate between the two cultures. Having an underdeveloped racial identity while living in a racialized society is detrimental to one's sense of self. The Linsanity phenomenon was explosive because it spoke to the deep desires of numerous Asian Americans who have been struggling with their racial identity for a long time. Jeremy was neither a stereotypical professional athlete nor a stereotypical Asian. Jeremy represented a new, more holistic Asian American persona that shatters social stereotypes while incorporating the best of both Asian and American cultures.

As race is still an undeniably powerful social reality, a healthy, stable racial identity is a sign of a mature and well-differentiated sense of self. In addition, embracing racial identity is important for spiritual formation and Christian discipleship among Asian Americans, helping us become morally sensitive to the reality of racial discrimination and injustice prevalent in US society. So, how can Asian Americans best cope with racism while critically incorporating both cultures? What does Scripture say about these vexing and challenging problems for Asian Americans? I want to examine these questions from three angles: how biblical figures dealt with questions of identity while living as a religious and cultural minority; what the Bible says about particular cultures such as "Asian"; and how these two issues are related to God in the Bible.

BIBLICAL RESPONSES

The question of identity is central to Scripture. Both individual biblical figures (such as Abraham, Jacob, Moses, Daniel, and Esther) and the nation of Israel as a whole struggled with the question of identity as they lived as members of a minority group in alien lands. In the case of Abraham, his very response to God's calling contained in it an acute threat to his identity. In a historical time when one's identity was derived from his or her tribe or clan, Abraham was told by God to leave his father's house and his native land, to go to a new place—meaning to give up the old identity and seek a new one. During his stay in Canaan, he was called a Hebrew, a person from the other side of a river, an alien. Additionally, because he had no son, he struggled with his identity as a married male in a culture where male identity was defined by fatherhood.

Moses, too, struggled with his identity. Though raised as a prince of Egypt, he was originally a member of the Hebrew people, a despised and oppressed minority group in the country. He grew up in a conflicting situation, with a princess of Egypt as his legal mother, but a Hebrew woman, his own biological mother, as his wet nurse. One sees similar struggles in the lives of Daniel, Mordecai, and Esther, who were caught between two cultures. While accepting certain elements of the Babylonian or Persian cultures (new names, languages, and statuses), they preserved certain aspects of the Jewish culture as a sign of solidarity with their people in exile and as a symbol of their dignity. Consequently, a healthy, mature sense of identity developed through the dialectic balance between their ongoing critical engagement with a dominant alien culture and Jewish culture.

The Apostle Paul was a Jew with Roman citizenship in a diaspora community. He was extremely conversant with both the Jewish tradition and Greco-Roman culture. While declaring there is neither Jew nor Gentile in Christ, the Apostle Paul himself was firmly rooted in Jewish identity to the extent that he writes in Romans 9:1–4: "I speak the truth in Christ—I am not lying, my conscience confirms it through the Holy Spirit—I have great sorrow and unceasing anguish in my heart. For I could wish that I myself were cursed and cut off from Christ for the sake of my people, those of my own race, the people of Israel."

Many other biblical stories portray how ancient Israel and early Christians survived as a religious and social minority in hostile environments. While facing enormous social pressure to assimilate to dominant cultures, they managed to maintain their identity without resorting to isolation or sectarianism.

What do their stories mean for Asian Americans? Who was (and is) the God these biblical figures encountered? These biblical figures found God as a personal and faithful God—the covenantal God who never deserted them despite their internal shortcomings or external challenges. They overcame adversities by trusting God. God's love was the inner protection against various dehumanizing forces pressing against them. They freely carried their emotions to God and found courage and hope as their new identity gradually grew out of their personal, covenant relationship with God.[4] This personal love of God is crucial for Asian Americans because, as was mentioned above, a major psychological challenge for Asian Americans is feeling that they are not loved for who they are, that love is conditional and they will be rejected. Once experienced, God's unconditional love will infuse a new sense of worth in them.

What is important is that God loves humans both unconditionally and particularly. Unconditionality and particularity are not mutually exclusive, but reinforce each other. God unconditionally loves each individual as he or she is created uniquely in God—a unique person with a distinctive temperament, personality, gifting, and passion. In God, one's skin color or

4. This changing identity of believers is evidenced in the stories of name changes of biblical figures. Abram became Abraham, just as Jacob became Israel, and Simon became Peter. Saul became Paul, after his dramatic conversion on the road to Damascus. A name is a primal marker of one's identity, and the change of one's name indicates the obtaining of a new identity in God.

facial characteristics have nothing to do with one's intrinsic worth or status. Nevertheless, God is not color blind; as the living God, God knows how a particular skin color, or ethnicity, functions in a society, and cares deeply. This is evidenced in the story of Exodus as God sides with the Hebrews against Egypt's abusive and ethnocentric behavior. How people treat others in terms of race, gender, and nationality matters to God, and God will not be passive in the face of injustice.

CULTURE

Many evangelicals mistakenly think that being a Christian means one ought to become culture-free or culture-transcending, able to deny all cultural influences. However, this is a very dangerous stance that borders on the heresy of Gnosticism (separating the spiritual reality from material, cultural, and historical reality by glorifying the former and demeaning the latter). On the contrary, Scripture offers a critical and refreshingly creative perspective on culture in general. God created everything good, including culture. Culture is a part of God's divine intention at creation. According to Genesis 2, the first human being, Adam, was a gardener whose work was to cultivate the land using his skills and wisdom. To be a Christian does not mean being supra-cultural or acultural. We cannot live outside of culture. Culture is a unique human activity, an expression of our creativity despite the distorting influence of sin. The only option is to critically engage what kind of culture we do have.

Every culture carries within it God's creational marks, witnesses to God's graceful presence with all of humanity, even though humanity is distorted by sinfulness. In history, no human culture has ever been entirely good or evil; culture is always ambiguous, a mixture of both good and evil, filled with gifts from God and distortions of those gifts. Therefore, every culture, including Asian and American cultures, needs to be reborn in Jesus Christ through the power of the Spirit. The ambiguous nature of culture calls for prudence and discernment in our cultural activities. Romans 12:2 reads: "Do not conform to the pattern of this world, but be transformed by the renewing of your mind. Then you will be able to test and approve what God's will is—his good, pleasing and perfect will."

In addition, human cultural expressions have been diverse throughout history. Just as God created animals, trees, birds, fish, and even humans of all kinds (Gen 1), human cultural experiences are also variegated. Race and ethnicity are simply aspects of such diverse cultural expressions. Racial and ethnic identity is an important part of living in any culture. It tells of our distinctiveness as humans—where we come from, what heritages we carry. To be a human means to be an embodied creature,[5] sexually (as male or female), culturally, and ethnically. Asian Americans embody their identities through their cultural heritages and experiences. Therefore, losing one's culture means losing an important part of one's identity. Scripture does not disregard cultural and ethnic identity. The book of Revelation affirms the value of cultural differences by reporting: "After this I looked, and there before me was a great multitude that no one could count, from every nation, tribe, people and language, standing before the throne and before the Lamb. They were wearing white robes and were holding palm branches in their hands" (Rev 7:9). The passage explicitly shows that God's final kingdom will be a gathering of culturally diverse groups of people, not one homogeneous cultural group.

In light of the above observations, Asian and American cultures have new meanings in God; neither is absolutely good or evil. Recentered in Christ, Asian Americans can take a constructive stance, neither uncritically rejecting or assimilating cultures but reappropriating them in sync with core biblical values. Just as they cannot blindly endorse authoritarian elements in Asian culture, they cannot glorify materialistic, individualistic American culture either. Rather they need to transform them in accordance with God's purpose and will,[6] and by doing so Asian Americans find they have even more to offer humanity. At the same time, it should be remembered that critical appropriation of both cultures requires an in-depth understanding of both cultures. Many young Asian Americans often have a very superficial, caricatured, or truncated understanding of their culture of origin; they judge their ethnic cultures only through their personal experiences with their parents, other immigrants, or depictions in mass media without having an appropriate cultural literacy.

---

5. Grenz, *The Social God and the Relational Self*, 277.

6. One may say that whereas God the creator is the source of our culture, God the redeemer is the corrector and guider of our culture, and God the Spirit is the sanctifier and refiner of our culture.

CONCLUSION

Racial identity is an integral part of identity development for young people living in a racialized and/or racially pluralistic society. For Asian American Christians, this means that they are required to integrate "Asian" and "American" aspects of their identity around the "Christian" identity that Christ provides. To be an Asian American Christian is to come to terms with our Asianness and Americanness in Christ without being chauvinistic or exclusionary toward other groups. This means that we endeavor to understand both cultures as deeply as we can—to be both fully Asian and fully American in a manner analogous to the way that Jesus Christ was fully divine and fully human. For Christians, developing such a healthy sense of racial identity could be considered a process of personal sanctification, for it is to discern and overcome the negative aspects and influences of both cultures and create a new cultural reality in oneself.

There will be many ups and downs, trials and errors, as Asian Americans deal with the pains of the past as well as the uncertainties of the future. They find themselves constantly negotiating many aspects of their life—desires, expectations, jobs, love, friends, family, social norms, etc. Their Christian faith may sometimes conflict with their parents and with society. However, in pursuing a more holistic form of Christian faith Asian Americans will find many beautiful gifts: a coherent worldview that coordinates the competing values and demands on their life, a support group that understands and shares their difficulties and challenges, and, above all, a God who is a true friend and a faithful shepherd to protect and guide them in their struggles. Despite many challenges within and without, when Asian American Christians keep searching and growing in God, they will eventually find their distinctive identity in God and make a meaningful contribution to our society through their rich cultural heritages and experiences. And this is not far from what the Apostle Paul meant when he proclaimed: "So if anyone is in Christ, there is a new creation: everything old has passed away; see, everything has become new!" (2 Cor 5:17).

DISCUSSION QUESTIONS:

1. What is cultural identity (racial, ethnic, gender) and how does it affect our personal and social life as Christians?

2. What particular challenges do young Asian Americans experience in their identity development, and why?

3. The author asserts, "To be a Christian does not mean being supra-cultural or acultural." What does he mean by this, and do you agree or disagree?

4. What resources does Scripture provide for healthy bicultural identity formation? Share examples from the Bible.

7

SEX

KIRSTEN S. OH

The recent K-Pop sensation, "Oppa'n Gangnam Style," went viral as soon as it was released on YouTube in July 2012, and as of August 2018, the music video has been viewed over 3.2 billion times. Named by *The Guinness Book of World Records* as the most "liked" video on YouTube, it has garnered several music and video awards and has spawned numerous parodies. The beat and music swept the world, making the pop celebrity Psy (Park Jae-sang) an international sensation whose music was dubbed a "force for world peace" by the former UN Secretary General, Ban Ki Moon. The lyrics flaunt the Gangnam District of Seoul and its lavish, rich, and charmed lifestyle. The song also ridicules the "posers" who want to look rich and famous, while it praises his girlfriend as classy and quiet (while knowing when to get wild and sexy).

The music video presents a highly sexualized form of a pelvic-thrusting dance along with suggestive invisible horse riding and lassoing. This song and the enticing music video have many contradictions, jumping from one scene to another in an erratic manner, which in many ways reflects the "postmodern young people [who] reside in a milieu of contradictions that do not reduce to neat explanations."[1] A shocking element of the video is that sexuality, including homoeroticism portrayed in parts of the

1. Also, for a contextual theological analysis of this video, see Cheah and Kim, *Theological Reflections on "Gangnam Style."*

music video, is no longer a taboo subject in a society that traditionally has been shrouded in the Confucian, shame-based heritage of East Asia that forbade any public display or discourse about sexuality. These traditional cultural values continue to challenge the increasing sexualization of the sociocultural milieu. Similar contradictions and challenges also are at play in the US between traditional religious beliefs and an eroticizing socio-cultural milieu. Given this complex dichotomy between traditional moral views on sexuality and a modern cultural shift, what sexual challenges do Asian American Christian college students and young adults face in these social contexts?

UNPLUGGED: REALITIES OF ASIAN AMERICAN CHRISTIAN COLLEGE STUDENTS AND YOUNG ADULTS

The rampant exposure to sexuality through multiple forms of media and the surrounding cultures is most often met with stoic silence within Asian American Christian families. In my conversations with Asian American Christian college students and young adults, I see a common pattern: Asian American parents avoid talking with their children about sex unless compelled by a crisis or coerced by school curricula. Even when coerced into "the talk," what follows is a simple mandate that sex before marriage is wrong and that one should "save" themselves for their marital partners, period. This message echoes throughout most Asian American churches that college students and young adults attend.

These Asian American churches often teach a strict notion of sexual-ity with language of purity, chastity, and holiness; abstinence until marriage is the only appropriate practice for Christians. These churches are partial to the traditional Christian morality, and suspicious of sexuality in general. Similar sexual convictions can be found throughout the history of Chris-tianity. For instance, St. Augustine, the bishop of Hippo, noted that sexual pleasure, even in marriage, impeded the pursuit of obedience and faithful-ness to God, and celibacy was considered the higher choice.[2] Under the influence of this negative approach to sexuality, Asian American churches and moral conservatives in other Christian communities alike have stressed the maintenance of "virginity." The "thou shalt not" aspect of sexuality gives

---

2. This "suspicion" toward sexuality is prevalent throughout the church history, in-cluding Clement of Alexandria, Origen, Athanasius, Chrysostom, and others. See Clapp, *Tortured Wonders,* 51–58.

the false impression that sex is "dangerous" or "dirty," but suddenly it must transform into something beautiful and sacred upon marriage.

There are socio-relational problems with demonizing sexuality. One of the results of such maligning is that some conservative Christian college students and young adults, caught between sexual desires and moral demands, may blur the lines of sexuality just enough to maintain technical virginity and the label of "purity." For example, they will rationalize that oral sex is acceptable since it does not involve penile-vaginal penetration, which is what they think counts as losing one's virginity. Students may push the envelope of sexual activity in an environment where clear boundaries are not present as they continue to ask, "How far can I go without losing my virginity?"[3] A Korean-American college student confesses:

> I believe sex is sacred and it needs to be held until marriage. This message was drilled into me from my family and church. But, when passionate feelings come, I am haunted by images in porn, sexualized music videos, and scenes from movies. More than that the images of my high school boyfriend and what we did sexually haunts me with shame. Don't get me wrong, we never had sex, but we did everything right up to it. If I didn't stop him, I would not be a virgin right now.

While the message from family and church was able to halt escalating bodily passions, according to the student, psychological and emotional realms are constantly bombarded by our sexualized culture of music, media, and Internet porn. A Japanese-American young adult agreed:

> I wish we didn't have that type of message [abstinence only] from my church, because it gave me the freedom to do everything up to having intercourse. It almost gave permission for all the other things leading up to sex. Not only that, I wanted to get married with my high school girlfriend as soon as my parents allowed it, so I can have intercourse.

These statements reveal the menacing sense of guilt that comes from sexual acts and the shame that invades the essential goodness of one's personhood. The statements also demonstrate the clear relational connection as Asian American young adults "tend to be more collateral in their relationships with people" than Anglo Americans.[4] That is, Asian Ameri-

---

3. For further reading, see Halpern-Felsher et al., "Oral Versus Vaginal Sex."

4. Sue and Sue, *Counseling the Culturally Diverse*, 202.

can Christian young adults maintain a communal sense of responsibility to uphold the messages they hear from their parents and churches. They may not necessarily voice their struggles to their parents or church leaders, but they strive to live by the messages they have received from them. These collateral, communal relationships contrast with the dominating North American cultural milieu regarding sex that is often characterized by hyper-individualism.

In both of the confessions above, while church and family relationships formed the individuals' reservations about having sex outside marriage, the messages from church and parents were interpreted as giving permission to every other sexual act. However, some feelings of shame and/or guilt after these other sexual acts remained. The Asian American cultural milieu in which these young adults find themselves is born out of the stoic chastity and sacrificial service that has endured throughout history in most Asian cultures, and is concomitantly reinforced by evangelical sexual ethics.

THE ASIAN AMERICAN CULTURAL MILIEU

The developmental stage of young adulthood along with collegiate culture can be summed up by the word *exploration*, which continues to feed into the formation of one's identity.[5] In conjunction with exploration, conservative sexual ethics, or the behavioral codes built upon "enduring, basic beliefs that typify cultures," are a part of the identity formation present in the young adult, collegiate development phase.[6] These convictions are usually formed through familial or institutional relationships, e.g., through unconscious cultural influence, church teachings, family expectations, etc.

For East Asian Americans, Confucianism deeply shapes these conscious/unconscious cultural convictions. According to Confucius, the roots of a woman's greatest virtues are maternal rectitude, purity and deference, chastity and appropriateness. Confucianism took various forms in East Asia, and in particular places like Korea, the adaptation of these virtues was enforced to such a degree that the children of widows who remarried were denied government office, while the families of those widows who committed suicide after their husbands' deaths were financially rewarded

---

5. Systematic theologian James McClendon defines culture as a "set of meaningful practices, dominant attitudes, and characteristic ways of doing things that typify a community (or a society or a civilization)." McClendon, *Systematic Theology* vol. 3, 50.

6. McClendon, *Systematic Theology* vol. 3, 50.

with lifetime tax-exempt status. Such reverence for sexual abstinence was especially administered during the Chosun dynasty (from the fourteenth to the nineteenth century).

In this way, while the definition of purity may vary within East Asia, one pervasive emphasis of the conservative sexual ethics espoused by Confucius is the importance of female virginity. On ABC News, *20/20* reported that every year hundreds of women, including a large number of Asian-Americans, have reconstructive plastic surgeries to repair their hymens.[7] Although it is not a reliable marker of virginity since the hymen can easily be torn during active sports and other vigorous activities, the pressure to present oneself as a virgin by getting one's hymen repaired through surgery is an attempt to preserve the traditional mark of purity. The importance placed on female virginity may not be a part of the broader American cultural reality, but it still remains a requisite formality for numerous Asian American households.

Confucianism places restrictions on a man's body, as well; it is not to be used for his own pleasure, but rather to serve the community and "bring peace and order to society."[8] Confucius regarded "an active sexual life as depleting a man's limited vital essence and therefore exhorted men not to waste their creative bodily resources."[9] As such, sexual intercourse was reserved primarily for the purpose of procreation. Given the culturally conservative sexual ethics, it is no wonder Asian American families refrain from addressing sexuality.

In addition, the subject of homosexuality is avoided, perhaps even dismissed in Asian American homes, especially if the parents are religious. Boyoung Lee, a professor of religious education, posits that homophobia is a result of the Confucius-oriented preference for male bodies. She writes, "In a culture where men's bodies and sexuality are regarded as superior to those of women, any non-traditional form of sexuality is a danger to this well-established social system."[10] In other words, during sex between

7. Cited in Boyung Lee, "Teaching Justice," 409–10. In addition, see http://abcnews. go.com/2020/WomensHealth/story?id=123701.

8. Boyung Lee, "Teaching Justice," 410.

9. Insook Lee, "Homoeroticism," 77. Lee quotes Confucius: "The gentleman should guard against it in youth when the bold and chi [flow of life force] are still unsettled; he should guard against attraction of feminine beauty" (Analects of Confucius, 16:7). It is notable, though, kings or nobilities own more than one wife, even multiple concubines.

10. Boyung Lee, "Teaching Justice," 406, 408. According to Lee, Asian persons that identity as LGBT or another sexual minority encounter discrimination for both the

men a man's body takes the role of a woman's body, while in lesbian relationships male bodies are not present. In addition, such male-male or female-female relationships from a Taoist perspective not only violate the yin-yang principle of female-male energy but also serve no social purpose since procreation becomes impossible. As a result, homosexuality is forbidden or culturally maligned.

Strict religious moral understanding potentiates this cultural understanding, resulting in the biases against homosexuality held by most evangelical and Catholic Asian Americans Christians. Such an attitude is demonstrated not only through individual narratives, but also through research. For instance, in a qualitative focus-group research of Catholic LGBTQ Filipino-Americans, participants agreed that religion, specifically Catholicism, generally opposed homosexuality and that "Filipino, gay, and Catholic were competing identities that could not be reconciled."[11]

This Asian American cultural DNA is doubly reinforced by the teachings of purity and holiness in churches that tend to be morally conservative. These teachings of purity, whether through "Silver Ring Thing" or "True Love Waits" campaigns, reinforce virginity through pledges and purity rings.[12] The twofold conservative sexual ethics of Asian culture and religion make any conversations about sexuality difficult, if not impossible. As Lee aptly puts it, the synergistic conservative sexual ethics may be, "where culture and Christianity become mutual malformers."[13] Nevertheless, familial, peer, and religious institutional relationships become the bearers of conservative sexual ethics that perpetuate traditional, collective Asian values contributing to Asian American women's and men's sexual suppression. This cultural milieu generates significant dissonance for Asian Americans living within the hyper-sexualized culture of North America in which virginity is frequently perceived as something to lose rather than to save.

---

sexual and racial aspects of their personhood from the Asian community. In fact, any kind of sexuality apart from heterosexuality is seen as Westernization and abandoning one's ethnic heritage. The notion of the preference for male bodies can also be noted from the New Testament culture of the ancient Greeks and Romans.

11. Nadal and Corpus, "'Tomboys' and 'Baklas,'" 5. LGBTQ is the more secret taboo subject in the Asian American context. As a note, Queer theologians would argue that gender and sexual identity are not the ultimate status. Instead conversion and subsequent baptism opens all to the hospitable embrace of the people of God. For an Asian American queer theological framework, see Cheng, "Multiplicity and Judges 19."

12. Freitas, *Sex and the Soul.*

13. Boyung Lee, "Teaching Justice," 413.

CAUGHT IN BETWEEN: SEXUALITY AND CARE OF
SEXUAL BODY PARTS

Multiple studies conducted in locations across North America showed that Asian North Americans begin sexual intercourse later in life, receive sex education at an older age, are less likely to desire children out of wedlock, and are less sexually promiscuous than their Caucasian counterparts.[14] Not surprisingly, the level of acculturation to the North American culture influences one's understanding of and engagement in sexual activity. A study of Chinese-American college students and young adults in Northern California exhibited "a positive correlation between the level of acculturation to the US and engagement in premarital sexual intercourse, and those Chinese Americans dating only Caucasian Americans consistently had more sexual experience than those dating only Chinese Americans."[15]

Additionally, a study conducted at a college in Southern California discovered that both Asian Americans and Caucasian Americans "who were less conventional (they were less religious, and more disposed to engage in variety of risk-taking behaviors) endorsed casual sex (sex without love or commitment)" and had more sexual experience.[16] The intriguing conclusion of the second study was that even though Asian Americans might hold similar attitudes toward casual sex as the surrounding American cultural forces, they engage significantly less in sexual intercourse. One of the reasons is that although family relationships are less determinative as individuals move from early to late adolescence as their autonomy increases, Asian American college students and young adults are still influenced by their parents' disapproval of casual sex.

The conservative sexual ethics of the Asian American family and church see chastity as the foundation for sexuality. Unfortunately, while the abstinence-only programs that hyped "virginity pledges" with purity rings may have resulted in fewer teen pregnancies, it fostered a proliferation of oral and anal sex to maintain "technical virginity" and did little to reduce promiscuity and sexually transmitted infections/diseases.[17] In other words,

14. Tong, "Acculturation," 560."

15. Okazaki, "Influences of Culture," 35–36.

16. McLaughlin et al., "Family."

17. Balswick and Balswick, *Authentic Human Sexuality*, 146. One study showed that "adolescents perceive oral sex as less risky, more beneficial, more prevalent, and more acceptable than vaginal sex." The study recommends education about oral sex—"the potential health, emotional, and social consequences and methods to prevent negative

while vaginal penetration is delayed in these Asian American young adults, most of them jettisoned the intent of the moralistic message of both their families and churches. The letter of the law (the literal application of the message) may be intact, but the spirit of the law (the intent or purpose of the message) is greatly compromised. The conservative sexual ethics of "thou shalt's" and "thou shalt not's" are easily abandoned when sexual activity can be used to satisfy emotional needs, to control or coerce someone, and/or for simple bodily pleasure.[18] Instead of this abandonment, I offer an alternative: covenantal Christian sexual ethics that emerge from a reflective, cultural, and theological response to sexuality.

COVENANTAL CHRISTIAN SEXUAL ETHICS: A BIBLICAL AND THEOLOGICAL RESPONSE

I teach a course titled "Christian Values and Human Sexuality" at a Christian liberal arts college and have the privilege to perceive the worlds of Christian college students through their reflection journals. When I point to research that many Christian emerging adults today are struggling between their intellectual integrity and their faith, between social sciences and Christianity, and between compassion and holiness, the students in my class also show a similar attitude. They want to hold these seemingly contrasting pressures in tension rather than choose one over the other.[19] As far as sexual ethics is concerned, they want to figure out a constructive way that respects both openness and faithfulness, compassion and holiness.

I had similar experiences as a young adult. Sex was ubiquitous in my surrounding American cultural milieu, not unlike today: steamy movie scenes, access to porn, racy music lyrics, and more. Yet I did not receive "sex education" from the public high school I attended or from my parents. I had to figure out the birds and the bees through piecing together conversations with peers. Without much reflection on why abstaining from sex was right, I kept a moral and pious conservative ethic of no sex before marriage as my familial, cultural, and religious relationships demanded. I

---

outcomes for all sexual activities, including non-coital behaviors such as oral sex"—in order to help adolescents make informed sexual decisions, according to Halpern-Felsher et al., "Oral Versus Vaginal Sex," 845, 850.

18. Halpern-Felsher et al., "Oral Versus Vaginal Sex," 849.

19. See http://religion.blogs.cnn.com/2013/07/27/why-millennials-are-leaving-the-church/

compliantly clung to this purity model to safeguard my psychological and physical health against the risk and complexities of being sexually active until I married in my mid-thirties. Some of my peers also subscribed to this conservative approach, which similarly promoted a negative, fear-based adherence to a strict rule. Failure to maintain purity meant sustained guilt and shame that caused emotional and even physical distancing from families and/or churches. The complexities of familial and religious moralities that often clash with cultural laxity, therefore, require a more reflective and nuanced sexual ethics.

Is there an approach that honors God in the midst of one's desires? This question proves to be a challenge, since the Asian context and the conservative Christian context seem to confirm similar conservative sexual ethics of purity, while the larger North American popular culture not only pushes against these ethics but seeks to eradicate it. In order to develop an authentic sense of self and continual development of sexual ethics, how then shall we engage these culture-laden clashes, conflicts, and contradictions? Developmental psychologist Robert Kegan proposes a helpful evolutionary model of identity that is built upon a meaning-making process that includes the dynamics of confirmation, contradiction, and continuity.[20] Kegan writes that a healthy way to navigate the contradictions, in this case among the hypersexualized cultural milieu, the conservative Asian cultural values, and the traditional biblical norms, is to integrate new meaning that merges both "old" convictions and "new" cultural realities to ensure continuity.[21] Incorporating both familial/religious and cultural constructs of meaning integrates the existing default frameworks into new ideas and realities.

While this process of integration may seem linear, that is progressing directly from the past to the present, the process is perhaps more cyclical, especially for those who are forming both their Christian and Asian American identities. Peter Phan explains it well in his understanding of "anthropology of time":

> We who live in time do not experience the past as something irretrievably lost and gone but as truly present, effectively shaping our identity and our destiny . . . . In this human time, the past is

---

20. Kegan, *The Evolving Self,* quoted in Boyung Lee, "Teaching Justice," 417.
21. Kegan, *The Evolving Self,* quoted in Boyung Lee, "Teaching Justice," 417.

gathered up and preserved in our *memory*, and the future is anticipated and made real in our *imagination*.[22]

Employing the framework of Phan's anthropology of time, one can hold the old (Asian/religious) reality while looking towards the new (emerging adult/collegiate) reality with equal tenacity to imagine and live into the future. One may experience a creative space to traverse both cultures by embracing the past to shape the future. Discernment becomes inextricable in this process of anthropology of time. In this space of discernment, one may question what parts of the old and new cultures must be retained and which can be rejected. For instance, there may be some parts of Asian and traditional church cultures to hold (respect and honor in collective communities), while there may be some parts to reject (systems of power and androcentric hierarchy). While we tenaciously hold on to the cultures that have formed the various aspects of our identity, we continue to engage the present culture within a community of people committed to reimagination and cultivation of a nuanced theology of sex through reflective reading of the Bible.

By employing Kegan's evolutionary model and Phan's anthropology of time, critical engagement with the contradictions between the current cultural influences and long-held moral influences become possible. For instance, a male Chinese American college senior searchingly questions the hypersexualized contexts in mass media that stand in paradox to his own sense of Asian and Christian cultural standards:

> Why does the [North American] culture so highly sexualize anything and everything? What relevance does a girl in a bikini, wearing barely anything, have in an advertisement for a fast food chain? It would be interesting to listen to the actual marketing conversation that sought to boost sales at the expense of exploiting women sexually. I would be equally perplexed by the people who saw these advertisements without batting an eye (I am guilty of this). There is something bizarre concerning culture and society that if it appears on billboards, TV, movies, and media, then it must be okay. For example, when Miley Cyrus' song, "Wrecking Ball" was first released, there was so much buzz surrounding the music video for its immodesty and exposure. Despite it all, if you were to ask someone about the music video today, people may still voice their opinions of Miley Cyrus but that initial shock of the video would have subsided as they have accepted the obscene.

22. Phan, "Betwixt and Between," 128–29.

Here, the student becomes aware of the contradiction between what he sees in mass media and his default cultural understandings, and he honestly confesses his own complicity with the hypersexualized mass media productions. A healthy move forward is to ask what default cultures are embedded in his Asian, familial, religious commitments that cause such reactions to these mass media examples he cites. Thoughtfully discerning and merging old convictions and critically accepting parts of the new cultural realities will help him assure the continual development of his own sexual ethics and identity.

While Kegan and Phan offer developmental continuation through discernment among competing contradictory cultures, for Christians, a theological framework remains critically important to any topic involving human sexuality. Here, the concept of covenant offers a meaningful relational bridge to sexuality. Covenant is one of the central concepts in both the Hebrew Bible and the New Testament, described in Scripture as the promise that connects the divine to both human communities and human relationships. God demonstrates what covenant looks like by God's sacrificial friendship with humanity through fierce fidelity under such covenant. God demonstrates covenant with "those whose concrete choices arise out of certain positive values [or positive regard for the other] that actually transcend culturally bound norms and politically enforced laws."[23]

In human-to-human relationships, covenant is between two equal parties who agree to abide together within set terms. A few of the descriptions of covenant in Scripture point to the bond between friends like Jonathan and David (1 Sam 20), an oath between an individual to a community like Joshua and the Gibeonites (Josh 9), and the pledge between individual within sexual relationships starting with Adam and Eve. Integrated with the sexual union is a command to be fruitful, multiply, and fill the earth (Gen 2:24). The reciprocal bonds in a covenantal framework represented in these relationships can overcome the limitations of conservative sexual ethics and sexual libertarianism. In sexual relationships, covenant rejects the communalism of Asian American culture and conservative Christian teachings that tend to be authoritarian and heteronomous. It also rejects the individualism of American culture that can lead to the use of sexual promiscuity to satisfy one's own need without regard for the other. Instead,

23. Mendenhall and Herion, "Covenant," 1201. In Hebrews, the writer emphasizes the faithfulness of God (10:23) "who above all is 'faithful,' whose promise can be utterly relied [upon]." Jesus Christ is the one who lived out that faithfulness and we as his disciples are called follow that example. Dunn, "Faith, Faithfulness," 422.

covenant points toward friendship based on love that considers another's needs before one's own. A part of that consideration begins with the awareness of one's own brokenness and insecurity. If left unchecked, these damaged parts of the self can potentially exploit the other for one's own need-fulfillment. Love is the capacity that can "lay down one's life for one's friends" (John 15:13) so that sexuality in love leads to a deeper relational connection rather than alienation.[24]

In other words, covenant with one another is not just an ideal; rather, it upholds a level of intimacy that is profoundly shared so that everyday choices are grounded in valuing the other in that relationship. The focus is not on sex, per se, but "on love, justice, desire, mercy, and equality in relating, including sexual relating."[25] These are not mere concepts, but values that tie into relationships between two bonded persons who commit to daily acts of fidelity, intimacy, tenderness, forgiveness, and humility. This kind of committed love stems from the relational aspect of covenant that risks a lifetime of mutual care, grace, joy, pain, embrace, vulnerability, and accountability in the mundaneness of daily life. In this sense, there is a tenacious commitment to sexual exclusivity reserved for that covenanted person with whom you desire to take the risk of relational and sexual mutuality. It is an adventure that carries no magical guarantees, but does entail a pledge that "opposes the promiscuous indulgence and/or predatory, exploitative expression of sexual desire" that promote individualistic desires for self-satisfaction.[26]

In this vein, the Christian ethicist Lewis Smedes insists that sexual intercourse between human beings happens at the level of ultimate intimacy: "Two bodies are never closer: penetration has the mystique of union, and the orgasmic finale is the exploding climax of one person's abandonment to another, the most fierce and yet most sensitive experience of trust."[27] In such relationships, deep friendship is at the core around which intimacy forms. That is, "one's experience of knowing and being known" is accompanied by the profound promise that covenants one to the other;[28] sexual intercourse consummates such covenant and deep friendship. And such

---

24. All quoted Scripture are from New Revised Standard Version.

25. Stuart, "Sexuality," 28.

26. Balswick and Balswick, *Authentic Human Sexuality*, 151.

27. Smedes, *Sex for Christians*, 122.

28. Balswick and Balswick, *Authentic Human Sexuality*, 88.

intimacy cannot be faked through just the physical dimension of merely "having sex."

Additionally, Christian ethicists Glen Stassen and David Gushee contend that sex in the context of covenant is not only enjoyable, but can be character forming: "Sex is not merely a moment of pleasure, like eating a candy bar, but a character-shaping action. And how a society practices its sexuality shapes not only the people in the society but the society itself."[29] The everyday choices one makes because of friendship with God and with one another forms that character. Covenantal relationship is the context where we can experience faithful intimacy that "transcend[s] life's failings and disappointments" in the commitment to mutual forgiveness, thereby offering healing from those failings and disappointments.[30]

The Gospel of John lays out the important topic of friendship throughout the book, culminating with Jesus' words to his disciples in John 15: 12–15:

> This is my commandment, that you love one another as I have loved you. No one has greater love than this, to lay down one's life for one's friends. You are my friends if you do what I command you. I do not call you servants any longer, because the servant does not know what the master is doing; but I have called you friends, because I have made known to you everything that I have heard from my Father.

The writer of John portrays a "model of friendship [that] emerges as a paradigm for the human vocation to embrace the other" resulting in people "who intend one another's well-being."[31] The Greco-Roman philosophy of Jesus' time made sacrificial friendship an ideal, so what Jesus said in John 10 about the Good Shepherd laying down his life for his sheep and in John 15 about a friend doing the same may not have been a new concept to his hearers. What is radical about Jesus' teaching about friendship in John 18 is that Jesus actually lays down his life and enacts the ultimate sacrifice in reality. Jesus' death on the cross stands in stark contrast to the Greco-Roman ideal in mere words. As such, Jesus' whole life is an incarnation of the ideal of friendship to protect sacrificially the beloved.

---

29. Stassen and Gushee, *Kingdom Ethics*, 291–92.

30. Stassen and Gushee, *Kingdom Ethics*, 291.

31. Hunt, *Fierce Tenderness*, 29.

Jesus' demonstration of true friendship rests on the goodness of such relationships in all kinds of friendships.[32] It is a fierce sacrificial tenderness that moves to protect the other. This relational wisdom from the Gospel of John inspires deep friendship. If sexual relationships can be built upon and continue to grow towards such deep friendship, Jesus' teaching about the kind of accountable, empowering, compassionate, hospitable, and justice-seeking—as well as justice-making—love in our deep friendship can also encompass our sexuality. Such love flies in the face of the current cultural sexual trend that portrays a cheap, sentimental, delusional love that lasts only through a brief pleasurable moment. This kind of love only pains and further alienates afterwards because while "we're up all night to get lucky" in order to hook up and "make my pulse react," love gets diminished as a "secondhand emotion" that is dismissed as a "sweet, old-fashioned notion."[33] Love as only a secondhand emotion that primarily revolves around no-strings-attached sexual pleasure is widely used in our current North American culture. Indeed, in this cultural milieu the heart *is* easily broken and definitely needs protection.

From the beginning, Scripture describes the beauty of human creation and the ensuing brokenness in Genesis. The inevitable search for reconciliation and healing designates the human quest for wholeness. Stassen and Gushee clarify it this way:

> The drama of Adam and Eve in Genesis 2 and 3 tells us something profound about ourselves: in our search for love, we are wounded, exiled, and alienated persons driven to find reconciliation, faithful community, and mutual affirmation that overcomes our alienation and isolation.[34]

Unfortunately, the North American cultural milieu perpetuates further alienation and isolation:

---

32. There are those who choose celibacy for vocation's sake in Christian life and those who remain single for manifold reasons. Those who are single also are fulfilled in their own understanding of self and sexuality through these relationships of deep friendship that mirror the life of Jesus with his disciples. Meaningful forms of sexual expression, albeit different from sexual intercourse, are possible for those who are single. In early church history, the life of singleness was more often preferred, following the Pauline imperative in 1 Corinthians 7.

33. From "Get Lucky" released in 2013 by Daft Punk, and "What's Love Got to Do With It?" released in 1984 by Tina Turner.

34. Stassen and Gushee, *Kingdom Ethics*, 291.

> We can search in momentary relationships based on ability to at-
> tract that end when we find another more attractive, in the latter
> case, the search for reconciliation and community leads only to a
> deeper mistrust, to selfishness, self-seeking, and the drive to find
> what we are missing in life by impressing others rather than by
> loyalty to others. The result is a deeper alienation.[35]

Lest our lives lead to deeper alienation, such friendship compels us to reshape our consumerist culture that often mistakes sex as a self-satisfying commodity. We need a more robust theology that integrates a renewed bib-lical understanding of friendship with some aspects of conservative sexual ethics to build a covenantal Christian sexual ethics. We need to engage in a reflective work that continues our identity development in the face of contradictions through the evolutionary model, the cultural continuity through the anthropology of time, and the theological understanding of covenant.

The biblical and Christian teachings regarding sexual intercourse are not meant to deprive anyone of sexual pleasure, but to safeguard the sa-credness of such intimacy in the mysterious beauty of a profoundly healing friendship. As Christian disciples, this covenant model "enables Christians to steer a course between the rampant libertarianism of contemporary cul-ture and a disordered repression of desire."[36] This is the reimaged shape of sexuality to strive for in the midst of the quest for intimacy and connec-tion. In this sense, the human quest for healing makes every human being vulnerable and necessitates the assurance that sexual partners undertake a covenantal risk toward sacrificial mutual care. These aspects of intimacy, fidelity, character formation, and healing are what covenantal Christian sexual ethics entail.

HOW THEN SHALL WE LIVE?

As we simultaneously hold the past and the present cultures, we are shaped by our reimaged sexual intimacy through fidelity within a covenant. In turn, how we live out our sexuality continues to shape our character and to promote our healing. Chastity, defined by Christian ethicist Lauren Winner as the "commitment to having sex in its proper place" as a single or a mar-ried person, is one of the ways we presently live out our sexuality in order

35. Stassen and Gushee, *Kingdom Ethics*, 291.

36. Sarah Coakley's exhortation for Christian discipleship in Stuart, "Sexuality," 28.

to live into fidelity within a covenant relationship in the future.[37] With this definition, Winner attests to the power of God's grace to restore us from failed sexual morals to renewed chastity. In this way, fidelity in covenant will go beyond the moralistic ethic that instills the fear of losing "technical virginity"; rather, covenanted relationship that sacrificially values the other in true friendship will reclaim a theology of risk in order to take an adventure for a lifetime that will deepen trust and cultivate healing through vulnerability with a committed person.

As a young adult, you have the agency to choose who you are becoming in the context of your communities (family, friends, church relationships, etc.), and you have the ability not only to shape your own sexual character but also to shape the culture around you by making good, everyday choices as a covenanted disciple of Christ. Your collateral relationships can become communities of accountability where confessions of both temptations and mistakes can be shared. These relationships can be safe places to practice fierce tenderness and care by refraining from both exaggerating and minimizing sexual sin.[38]

Remember that God is there alongside each one of us and we are people of grace and compassion. Let your sexuality reflect your identity and worth as a person wonderfully and fearfully made by the one who created all humanity in God's own image. This God enlarges the boundaries of love in fidelity and in covenant so that we can risk being accountable, empowering, compassionate, hospitable, justice-seeking, and justice-making.

DISCUSSION QUESTIONS:

1. How does the biblical understanding of covenant speak to your Asian American hybrid existence that values collectiveness and individuality, respectively?

2. Regarding sexuality, what is one value from your Asian culture and one value from the present culture you inhabit that you want to hold onto tenaciously?

---

37. Winner, *Real Sex*, 134. This definition arises from the New Testament understanding of distorted sexuality: "fornication" and "sexual immorality"—Acts 15:20; 1 Cor 5:1, 6:13, 18: 7:2, 10:8; 2 Cor 12:21; Gal 5:19; Eph 5:3; Col 3:5; 1 Thess 4:3.

38. For more suggestions like this, see Balswick and Balswick, *Authentic Human Sexuality*, 157–58.

3. Given that sexual desire is natural and normal according to the Bible, what does fidelity (to God, to self, and to your partner) mean for your single life, and in what ways can chastity appropriately and healthily be expressed and/or practiced?[39] In other words, how would you express the degree of sexual intimacy that corresponds to the degree of commitment and fidelity in a relationship?

---

39. "It is important for singles to express themselves in wholesome ways as authentic sexual persons. The capacity to respond to others in a positive pleasurable way is congruent with a healthy sexuality. Physical expression requires self-awareness, knowledge, discipline and a godly value system." Balswick and Balswick, *Authentic Human Sexuality*, 155.

8

GENDER

Kirsten S. Oh

Memoirs of a Geisha was released in 2005 to critical acclaim. Nominated for six Academy Awards, the movie garnered three awards for Best Cinematography, Best Art Direction, and Best Costume Design. The movie was based on an historical novel of the same title by Arthur Golden, in which the narrative weaves a complex portrayal of love, honor, fidelity, and pain. Inherent in this widely disseminated story is the persisting Asian cultural stereotype of the subservient female and the dominant male. Based on a real-life story of a geisha named Sayuri, the first-person account of the memoir presents a girl whose life has spun out of control. During this vulnerable time of chaos, the young Sayuri falls in love with "Chairman," an older male of considerable wealth and power, who shows her kindness. She determines to become a geisha in order to meet the Chairman again someday and become a part of his life.

The narrative of *Geisha* epitomizes the stereotype of Asian girls pressured to become women who sacrifice their lives to gain or keep protection and affection. Similarly, men are pigeonholed into a dominant, strong, and powerful gender role. These gender roles are ubiquitous in most traditional patriarchal societies. In many Asian cultures, Confucianism has granted these roles an even stronger influence. However, such binary gender roles are not only scripted in the Asian cultures of yesteryear.

National Geographic's special issue dedicated to the "Gender Revolution" in 2017 notes that these gender roles, represented by color codes of pink for soft and sweet qualities in girls and blue for strong and masculine qualities in boys still dictate the lives of many Asians in China, India, Korea, and Japan. For instance, in this *National Geographic* issue, nine-year-old Fang Wang of China states, "Sometimes I secretly help my older brother [on the farm]. Mom whacks me when she finds out. She says that girls who do these things will grow calluses on their hands; then they become ugly."[1] The ongoing enforcement of these binary gender roles perpetuates harmful, implicit biases for each of the genders despite radical shifts in the understanding of gender roles among Millennials, who define roles more fluidly with multiple terms, layers, and complexities.[2]

Given Asian culture's gendered norms, how do Asian Americans negotiate their genders in the United States, amid a radical postmodern cultural shift, while their parents and ethnic communities reinforce binary gender roles? What stereotypical roles are forced upon Asian American women and men by cultural peer pressure? What does Scripture say about this issue? How do we negotiate this particular identity?

WHAT IS GENDER IDENTITY?

In order to explore gender roles, or "the outward way that people exhibit gender identity . . . deemed typical for girls/women and boys/men," the definition of gender identity, upon which gender roles are built, needs further explication.[3] "Gender identity" is embraced in both gender and developmental studies. The American Psychological Association defines gender identity as "one's sense of oneself as male, female, or transgender."[4] The related classification of "gender" refers to the attitudes, feelings, and behaviors of a person in reference to being gendered within a specific

---

1. In this special issue of *National Geographic*, Eve Conant spoke with eighty children in eight countries from the Americas to the Middle East, Africa to China. Conant, "I Am Nine Years Old," 35.

2. Henig, "Rethinking Gender," 52.

3. Delaney, "Gender Identity Development," 80.

4. *The Guidelines for Psychological Practice with Lesbian, Gay, and Bisexual Clients, adopted by the APA Council of Representatives, February 18–20, 2011.* The complexity of intersexual persons broadens the conversation beyond the binary gender construct of male and female. Additionally, some experience incongruence between their biological sex and their psychological/emotional identity as either female or male.

culture and the understanding of that culture's association with a person's physical, biological, and anatomic dimensions of being male or female. In short, gender identity is how one experiences oneself within the social and cultural aspects of being male or female. In North America, gender identity formation begins as soon as parents find out the biological sex of the child. Gender-specific, socially accepted norms of that particular gender are ingrained in them, even down to such details as the color of their infant's clothing: "pink for a girl and blue for a boy."[5]

In other words, gender identity is socially constructed to conform to one's biological sexual characteristics: both primary (having to do with reproductive organs) and secondary (having to do with other biological characteristics that develop during and after puberty). Studies show that gender identity is generally formed by the age of three, and that each particular identity continues to form based on the approval or disapproval of social influences like family, teachers, religious figures, mass media, and other factors in the child's life.[6] Therefore, expressions such as gender-specific ways of talk, movement, gesture, behavior, play, clothing, interests, and roles are culturally laden. For instance, girls play with dolls, kitchen sets, and vacuum cleaners to imagine being a housewife, while boys play with building blocks, trains, and cars to imagine being the breadwinner of a household.[7] In these ways, one's gender identity is articulated at all levels of formation: biological, sociological, cultural, and spiritual. While there are examples of exceptions to the general understanding of gender normative roles,[8] it seems that this social construction of gender has an implicit gen-

5. Although this classification of boys and girls into two distinct characteristics is normative, more research on the exceptions to the binary gender identity (genderqueer, transgender, intersex) shows the complexities beyond this classification. In fact, Facebook has fifty different options for gender identity. There is an increasing awareness of those who are exploring their gender identity beyond their biological gender, which is labeled the "third gender." A small population has the experience of having an emotional and a psychological identity that does not match one's biological sex, otherwise known as "gender dysphoria." Visit www.sexualidentityinstitute.org and/or see "Sexual Orientation and Gender Identity Development" in Laser and Nicotera, *Working with Adolescents*.

6. Weiler, *Codes and Contradictions*, 8. Additionally, age, ethnicity, race, sexuality, and social class influence the organization and meaning of gender.

7. See Balswick and Balswick, *Authentic Human Sexuality*, 15. A third gender is used for intersex and/or transgender persons and the concept of gender fluidity is considered normative in many cultures (see footnote below). I use the continuum of male-female identities for the purposes of this chapter.

8. For example, in the Independent State of Samoa, those who identify as "fa'afafine" are males who follow feminine-typical roles and behaviors and are sexually attracted

der bias and spans the world. From "China to Canada and Kenya to Brazil" when nine-year-old boys and girls "describe big dreams for future careers . . . the boys don't see their gender as an impediment, while the girls, all too frequently, do," according to research published in 2017.[9]

ASIAN/ASIAN AMERICAN AND GENDER PREFERENCES AND ROLES

These social constructions were evident in my family of origin. My mother, along with her entire family, converted to Christianity as a result of her physical healing when she was ten years old. She later married my father, the only person in his family who was a Christian, and a pastor at that. Both were passionate about serving God, and one way my mother hoped to serve God was to be a good witness to my father's unbelieving family by birthing a son. In her socially constructed world, the birth of a son would show her non-believing in-laws the greatness of God. However, when she gave birth to two girls in a row without bearing a son, she felt she had tarnished her witness of God's blessing.

Xinhong Yao, a professor of religion and ethics, explains that this response is bound up in Confucianism: "In the [Confucian] family, the primary virtues of a young woman were considered to be her filial piety towards parents and parents-in-law, assistance to her husband and education of her children."[10] This male-dominated hierarchy perpetuated binary gender roles that correlated with the principle of the universe. That is, "The correct place of the woman is within; the correct place of the man is without."[11] The notion that woman's place is within explains one of the terms for wife in the Korean language, 안사람 (the inside person). This view of the wife as the one who devotes her life to the order of the household and the education of her children is shared in China and Japan. In this patriarchal philosophy, the male is the dominant "yang" while the female is the subservient "yin."

---

to males. For the Samoan culture, these men are considered "normal" in their gender identification. Delaney, "Gender Identity Development," 86–87.

9. Conant, "I Am Nine Years Old," 32.

10. Yao, *An Introduction to Confucianism*, 183.

11. Wilhelm, *Confucius and Confucianism*, 570; Yao, *An Introduction to Confucianism*, 184.

Though a devout Christian, my mother's Confucian-laden cultural understanding of her gender only legitimized self-respect and honor in the context of sacrificially raising children, particularly a son. It is no wonder that my mother, along with many other Asian mothers and grandmothers, preferred boys and prayed fervently for a son; she was considered "blessed" when she finally birthed a son. Similarly, many Asian Americans have an unconscious preference for boys. This is not only due to their familial culture, but also to other societal cues such as Asian American friends, church structures, media, and the like. The intersection of gender and ethnic identity demonstrates the lingering effects of the Asian cultural norms. The common result of this intersection may be a division between personal, familial, religious, and cultural worlds as one seeks to construct a cohesive gender identity; this division may be seen through the following confessions of Asian American college students and young adults.

CONFESSIONS OF ASIAN AMERICAN COLLEGE STUDENTS AND YOUNG ADULTS

Gender roles have a lot of influence over young Asian Americans. Navigating the complex cultural terrains of being perpetual foreigners per their appearance, accepting their in-between identity of adolescent development, and inhabiting their Asian American cultures in their home and church, Asian American college students and young adults cling to similarities as they deliberate the vast contradictions.

The clash between being Asian and American is stated well in the words of three Asian American college students. A Japanese American college male recalls the following:

> When I was growing up, most boys pretty much liked the color blue or green. Also we all enjoyed playing contact sports, video games, watching movies with violence, or reading books along the same themes. Girls were the opposite. Girls' favorite color was always pink, if not it was a little bit weird. Also they all wanted horses or ponies and played with dolls. Girls generally didn't watch that many movies but would read a lot.

He contrasted this with his Japanese culture: "Japanese culture, in a lot of ways is similar to American culture except the way they dress. [Japanese] men generally dress a little more feminine than American men. Also men in Japan will wear a man purse as opposed to a backpack." A

Chinese-American college male noticed a similar trend while traveling throughout China, Hong Kong, and Taiwan for a month: "The majority of males didn't act, dress, or possess the [same] mannerisms as the typical 'masculine' American male." He added:

> I think we got a hint from the billboards sprawled across the country depicting the type of "boyness" of Asia—slender, fashionable, and longer hairstyles. I'm not saying every male embraces this stereotype but I think the culture in these countries uses certain means such as billboards to reinforce the definition of "boy-ness." I remember frantically begging my mom to go to Costco to buy me a couple pair of boxers because I did not want to face the ridicule of being teased for wearing that childish white underwear that looked like a baby's diaper. This began in 6th grade when everyone had to change in the locker rooms, and you would automatically be judged for wearing boxers or underwear. In high school, "boy-ness" would be proven by the girlfriend you had around your arms, the dominance you displayed in a sport, or the notoriety of your reputation. I played football for two years in high school and your "boy-ness" would either be proven on the field or in the locker room where there would frequently be wrestling matches. Looking back, it bewilders me as to why there was so much value placed in the most insignificant things.

Both of these stories resonate with the prevalent "flower boy" concept of recent Korean-dramas, which has changed the term "Oppa" from meaning an older brother or "honey" to a pretty boy or handsome male. In the above statements, the young adults describe different expressions of gender between Asian and American contexts, however, the binary roles of each gender remain the same.

On the other hand, an Asian American female young adult writes, "When I was growing up, 'boy-ness' and 'girl-ness' were complexly intertwined." Her own experience stands apart from the experience of her Japanese American grandparents, particularly in their understanding of gender roles:

> I have stories from my mom about my Japanese grandmother, and her role within her family before her husband died and was diagnosed with Alzheimer's. My grandmother was to be mother to her children and cared for the workers, who worked with my grandfather, and someone who ran the household [while] cleaning and cooking. My grandmother was to be a faithful wife and mother before working, and should submit to her husband. My

grandfather was to be the breadwinner for the family, and did not have much responsibility with the children. The males received better treatment as compared to the females. American practices of gender expectations are different from many cultures, including the Japanese viewpoint. In American culture, the woman is expected to rear the children and maintain the household, and often simultaneously keep a job. I believe that the Japanese culture of my grandparents would view American gender differences negatively. There was a sense of pride that the man was able to support the family, and that is how many families functioned then.

Like other Millennials, many Asian American college students and young adults may personally embrace an egalitarian understanding of their own identity and role. Maria Kohlman notes, "Most recent research in this area of scholarship indicates that younger cohorts of men and women alike aspire to more egalitarian relationships in which gender roles are increasingly fluid, and work and family responsibilities are more flexibly divided."[12] However, when they return home from college during breaks, they often revert back to culturized, family-systems–driven roles based on gender. In college, another competing set of gender roles might prevail, both in their classrooms and among their friends. Since social and cultural cues are not uniform due to various incongruent gender roles, unhealthy levels of identity confusion during one's adolescent and/or young adult years can impede healthy gender identity development. This particular life stage proves critical for the development of healthy gender identity development, as most college-age students want to make significant relationships with persons of all genders.[13] For Asian Americans, the clash between familial cultural understandings of gender and the dominant cultural understanding of gender may require further negotiating to find one's own gender roles apart from the culturally bound roles of either being Asian or American. Unfortunately, Asian American gendered stereotypes further perpetuate the complexity of navigating this process.

ASIAN AMERICAN GENDERED STEREOTYPES

The issue becomes more complex with the Asian American gendered stereotypes promoted by the Western media. Essentializing stereotypes

12. Kohlman et al., *Notions of Family*, xv.
13. See Erikson, *Identity and the Life Cycle*.

of Asian Americans play a significant part in the politics of gender roles. Patricia Williams argues the difference between good visibility and bad visibility, in *The Alchemy of Race and Rights: Diary of a Law Professor*: "Bad visibility involves hypervisibility, objectification, making a spectacle, stereotyping. Good visibility, on the other hand, involves a recognition of individuality."[14] In our mass and social media culture, more often than not, Asian Americans have bad visibility—often objectified or pigeonholed into certain stereotypes.

Both male and female Asian Americans fall under the "model minority" category of an Asian nerd. This stereotype presents both genders of Asian Americans as super smart, straight-A students, and incredibly industrious, upwardly mobile persons, whose only focus is getting into Harvard or Yale. With myopic focus on academic excellence or rigid work ethic, they lack social abilities.

Asian American men are frequently described as less attractive, sexless, and lacking in social skills. For instance, Asian American men have been routinely "emasculated and feminized in the dominant cultural discourse" in the US mass media as waiters, cooks, servants, and nerds with only a few exceptions of gangsters with martial art skills.[15] Although Asian American men like Jeremy Lin, the basketball phenomenon, Daniel Dae Kim, the actor who plays a motorcycle-riding Hawaii 5-0, and Harry Shum Jr., the singing and dancing heartthrob in *Glee*, have recently challenged the dominant stereotypes, the objectified stereotypes still remain.

A popular female stereotype is the "good" Asian female—subservient, reverential, and docile—not unlike the depiction of the geisha, Sayuri. This China (porcelain) doll stereotype invites the idea of the childlike, innocent Asian woman who needs to be dominated and taken care of. The model minority myth reinforces these passive, feminine, non-assertive images of Asian Americans. On the other hand, another female stereotype is the exotic, erotic, and sensual Asian woman and her assumed lack of morality, which was a part of the justification for anti-Asian sentiments and, subsequently, the Chinese Exclusion Act of 1882.

Mental health professionals have argued that, although these are mere pop culture stereotypes, the images not only influence how others see

14. Williams, *The Alchemy of Race and Rights*; Phinney, "Ethnic Identity and Acculturation," 63.

15. Chang and Yes, "Using Online Groups to Provide Support," 635. A stereotype that refers mainly to Asian American males: a martial arts expert/fanatic like Bruce Lee or Jackie Chan.

Asians, but how Asian Americans view themselves and other Asian Americans. These stereotypes significantly affect, among other things, dating attitudes and partner selection for or against Asian Americans.[16] The largest Facebook dating app, AYI, tracked 2.3 million heterosexual interactions and found dating is highly racialized across particular gender lines: "Most men prefer Asian women (except Asian men), while most women (except black women) are most drawn to white men. Interestingly, the researchers of the dating app found men from all racial groups tend to prefer women from races other than their own."[17]

In their research on Asian American mental health, Sue and Morishima found Asian American men are often characterized as quiet, timid, shy, and hardworking, very similar to that of the model minority, nerd stereotype.[18] Due in part to this stereotype, Asian American women viewed white men as more physically and/or sexually attractive than Asian American men, even though they were viewed as someone who can share their mutual traditions, customs, language, and family expectations. On the other hand, white men describe their views of Asian/Asian American women with the words "introverted, quiet, obedient, and observe traditional sex roles," which are very stereotypical descriptions that perpetuate "yellow fever." Not surprisingly, in a study conducted by Fujino, no Asian/Asian American women described themselves in these subservient ways.[19]

To counter these stereotypes and to develop a neutral stance that permits "good visibility," one must detect the often gendered and racialized stereotypes as "bad visibility" and remember not to project these characterizations onto others and/or themselves. An understanding of "hybridity" aids in cultivating a non-essentialized individuality that leads to "good visibility." Asian Americans live in a hybrid culture and space. According to Sang Hyun Lee, "To construct a hybrid Asian American identity in American society is, first of all, to resist the essentialized idea either of America or Asia."[20] Just as we straddle the spectrum of being Asian and American, we

---

16. Sue and Morishima, *The Mental Health of Asian Americans*, 117.

17. http://www.dailymail.co.uk/sciencetech/article-2511049/Online-dating-app-reveals-race-matters-romance.html, accessed August 21, 2014.

18. http://www.dailymail.co.uk/sciencetech/article-2511049/Online-dating-app-reveals-race-matters-romance.html, accessed August 21, 2014.

19. Fujino, "Extending Exchange Theory"; cited in http://sitemaker.umich.edu/psy457_lamyiu/stereotypes_and_dating_attitudes, accessed January 31, 2013.

20. Sang Hyun Lee, *From a Liminal Place*, 112.

also straddle the spectrum of the male and female roles as embodied Asian Americans. What, then, might offer a better alternative?

MADE IN GOD'S IMAGE: MALE AND FEMALE

An alternative gender identity, from which our gender roles stem, comes from the biblical understanding of identity. There are several gender identity narratives in Scripture, and of those Genesis 1–2 and Galatians 3 offer alternative discourses. Both of these texts offer a dynamic, multidimensional construct that involves a fluidity of one's gender identity in which individual reality is constructed and reconstructed rather than being forced into stagnant, rigid roles. The narrative of Jacob demonstrates such fluidity over one's lifetime.

Genesis 1 contains a poetic declaration on the image of God. Genesis 1:27 reads: "So God created humankind in his image, in the image of God he created them: male and female he created them." Both men and women bear the divine image. Both genders, and the spectrum that exists around them, are needed in order to complete the image of God; the radical notion of this shared, interdependent humanity represents God's image.[21] In Genesis 2, God empathetically describes Adam's status of being alone as not good and forms a "helper" or a partner from the side of the human.

The male and female genders are distinguished particularly in verse 23 when the man rapturously bursts into poetry, "This is bone of my bones and flesh of my flesh. This shall be called a woman, for from a man was she taken."[22] Genesis 2 and 3 have historically been interpreted to legitimate male headship due to the woman being described as a "helper" and the first to succumb to the serpent's temptation.[23] However, Hebrew Bible scholar Gordon Wenhem asserts, "It is often suggested that the story of woman's creation from man's rib illustrates the meaning of this traditional kinship formula . . . . This formula sets man and woman on an equal footing as regards their humanity, yet sets them apart from the animals (Gen 19–20;

21. "Spectrum" signifies the movement away from just the binary structure of gender to a larger, expansive understanding of genders that include Christians who also are intersex, genderqueer, and gender nonconforming.

22. In Hebrew, *îš,* "man," and *iššāh,* "woman," are from the same root, with woman simply meaning "from man."

23. See Beattie, "The Theological Study of Gender," 39–40. Additionally, the word *helper* is used mostly to describe God: Exod 18:4, Deut 33:7, Ps 20:2, Ps 33:20, Ps 70:5, Ps 115:9, Ps 121:1.

also Gen 1:26–28)."[24] The rib signifies that the woman is neither above nor below the man, but they are side-by-side equals.

At first perusal, Galatians 3 appears to portray a completely different understanding of gender, eliminating the differences that Genesis 2 distinguishes so carefully. The Apostle Paul confidently declares, "There is no longer Jew or Gentile, there is no longer slave or free, there is no longer male and female; for all of you are one in Christ Jesus" (3:28). Noted as an eschatological vision of being "in Christ," the male or female couplet occurs with Jew or Gentile and free or slave. Rather than eliminating the differences, these three couplets might have been "a conscious attempt to counter the misdirected three blessings that appear at the beginning of the Jewish cycle of morning prayers: 'Blessed be He [God] that He did not make me a Gentile; blessed be He that he did not make me a boor [slave]; blessed be He that He did not make me a woman.'"[25] If this is the case, then embedded in this text is the preference for equality of all humanity, harkening back to the original intent of God's created order. The *Message* translation reflects this intent: "In Christ's family there can be no division into Jew and non-Jew, slave and free, male and female. Among us you are all equal. That is, we are all in a common relationship with Jesus Christ."[26] In Christ, we are a new humanity. This does not mean that ethnic, national, gender, social, or economic distinctions are eliminated; rather, they are transformed. The distinctions are no longer divisions of hierarchy or markers of blessed and cursed states. Here, Paul's teaching about gender roles calls for mutual edification and submission.

In the ministry of Jesus Christ, examples of gender equality are prominently displayed as Jesus crosses the gender boundary and befriends, affirms, serves, and raises women to equal status as men: the Samaritan woman (John 4) with whom he has the longest personal conversation recorded in the New Testament Gospels, Mary Magdalene (Mark 15 and Luke 8), and Mary and Martha (Luke 10, John 11), to name a few. In Christ, the male-female binary distinctions are liberated to equal standing so that spectrums of these identities become possible, stereotypes of racialized genders can be questioned, and the individual non-stereotypical selves of Asian American women and men are liberally expressed.

---

24. Wenham, *Genesis*, 70.

25. Longnecker, *Galatians*, 157.

26. Peterson, *The Message*, 1588.

Gender roles are represented fluidly in Scripture, even among Hebrew men as exemplified in the narrative of Jacob and Esau. These twin brothers, born to Rebekah and Isaac, display at first binary roles between what is considered masculine and feminine (Gen 25—28). Esau, ruddy, hairy, and more masculine from birth, becomes a skillful hunter who roams the wide fields of the countryside while Jacob, smooth-skinned and more feminine from birth, becomes a cook who contentedly stays home (Gen 25:26). One demonstrates the traditional skills and role of a man while the other the skills and role of a woman.

Jacob's narrative continues with Jacob leaving the home he loved. After he deceives his father into giving him the blessing that belongs to his older brother, Esau, by birthright, Jacob traverses to Paddan Aram and works for his uncle Laban as a shepherd (a position Rachel held according to Genesis 29:9). During this time, he takes on the masculine role of father to the twelve sons/tribes of Israel through his marriages with two sisters, Leah and Rachel (and their maidservants Zilpah and Bilhah). When the time comes for Jacob to head back to his homeland, Jacob pauses alone at the ford of Jabbok river the night before meeting Esau. There, Jacob wrestles with a man through the night and wins to gain a blessing: "Then the man said, 'You shall no longer be called Jacob, but Israel, for you have striven with God and with humans and have prevailed'" (Gen 32:28). It is clear that throughout his lifetime, Jacob assumes various roles from a cook, shepherd, husband, father, and wrestler, showing that gender identities and roles are fluid.

Although Esau's story is not as pronounced in the Genesis account, he seems to have maintained his masculine leadership identity, coming to meet Jacob with 400 men. However, his gender identity shift is revealed when he initiates the embrace when meeting Jacob: "But Esau ran to meet him, and embraced him, and fell on his neck and kissed him, and they wept" (Gen 33:4). Esau, the man's man, has become more tender and relational over his lifetime, running, embracing, kissing, and weeping at the sight of his long-lost brother. What is masculine and feminine are not represented in binary ways. Rather, they are fluid, especially as described in the narrative of Jacob and Esau.

HOW THEN SHALL WE LIVE?

A full understanding of these biblical texts offers a liberative, non-essential-ized, hybrid sense of gender identity around which Asian American college students and young adults can structure and restructure their gender roles as they negotiate various contexts. This alternative vision can underpin new practices of being a Christian, Asian American, gendered person. In contrast to both historical Asian and patriarchal Christian understandings of gender identities and roles, by reading Scripture through alternative lenses and holding onto the image of God as both male and female, Asian American young adults can grasp the preference of God to see all humanity as "made in God's image" and thus embrace the distinct particularities of their identities.

As a college student and a young adult, you have the ability to choose who you are becoming as you continue to form and reform a cohesive understanding of yourself, navigating the many competing worlds you inhabit. In relationships, may the hybrid nature of gender identity liberate you as you begin to form your own sense of identities and roles.

DISCUSSION QUESTIONS:

1. The beginning story of Jacob counters the cultured, gendered stereo-type of his time; Jacob is portrayed as a quiet man who cooked and dwelled in tents as opposed to Esau, who hunted and dwelled in the fields (Gen 25:27). Who are some other biblical characters that coun-tered their culture's gendered stereotypes? Study these persons and ask: Who were they? What difficulties did they encounter as non–gen-der-typical identities? How did they respond? Where did they find the resource or strength to do so? What do you learn from these persons?

2. How do the story of Jacob and other alternative biblical understand-ings of gender roles such as the stories of Deborah (prophet, judge, wife in Judges 4) or of Priscilla (teacher, evangelist, church-planter, pastor, wife in Acts 18) help you imagine an alternative visioning of your Asian American gender identities and roles? What other stories do you find helpful in envisioning the continuing development of your own gender identity and roles?

3. What mechanisms or practices will help you encounter gender stereotypes of Asian Americans in the media and/or from family that you might stop, notice, reflect, and counter with a more complex understanding of your particular gender identities and roles?

4. What are some ways you can remind yourself of your identity in Christ that encompasses all the strengths, gifts, and talents you possess while you also affirm the identity of others in Christ in order to more accurately discern your roles in your life and your work? In what ways can you imagine your particular gender roles changing and evolving within your lifetime with flexibility and fluidity?

9

MYTH OF MODEL MINORITY

JANETTE H. OK

When Amy Chua's *Battle Hymn of the Tiger Mother* first debuted, excerpts and reviews of the book along with interviews with its unapologetic author caused nothing short of a media sensation. Whatever your opinion is about the book or Chua's parenting style, one thing is certain: the idea of Asian Americans as the model minority continues to hold sway in the American public imagination. Here is the opening line of the memoir:

> A lot of people wonder how Chinese parents raise such stereo-typically successful kids. They wonder what these parents do to produce so many math whizzes and music prodigies, what it's like inside the family, and whether they could do it too. Well, I can tell them, because I've done it.[1]

After all, Chua's daughters serve as living proof that the image of Asian American youths as exceptionally successful is not just a stereotype but reality. Chua in some respects embodies the stereotypical image of the super competitive, ambitious, tireless, and sacrificial Asian mom, who channels all her energy and invests every possible resource toward the advancement

1. I am very grateful to SueJeanne Koh for her comments on earlier drafts of this manuscript.
Chua, *Battle Hymn of the Tiger Mother*, 3.

of her children. In other respects, she challenges stereotypes by writing a book in which she airs out her family's dirty laundry without cowering or backing down from telling her story as her story (her book, she claims, is a memoir not a manifesto). Chua concludes that the values that made America's founding fathers so great are the very same Chinese values she relentlessly strove to instill in her kids: extraordinary ambition, a tireless work ethic, and zero tolerance for self-pity or complaining.

You yourself may have been raised by parents who pushed and pressured you to excel academically and focus single-mindedly on doing whatever it took to get into a prestigious college.[2] Once in college, you may have been expected to secure a respectable, well-paying job or pursue graduate school while dating someone with a similar or superior educational pedigree. Your sacrificial and hardworking parents may have told you stories of other friends' kids who had "made it" as a well-intended but passive-aggressive reminder of their own aspirations for your success. You may feel like you fit some of the stereotypes of the model Asian American or like a glaring exception to the rule because you're just "average" and thus a disappointment to your family and society. For Asian Americans, success is not only measured by how we are perceived relative to other Asian Americans but also other racial-ethnic groups.

THE PRICE OF BEING EXCEPTIONAL

No matter where you stand in the spectrum of Asian American exceptionalism, being hailed as "America's greatest success story"[3] has its perils, pressures, and privileges. The model minority stereotype may seem to valorize Asian Americans for who we are, but it is as much about who we aren't. Frank Wu points out, that the term "model minority" itself necessitates the questions, "model of what?" and "model for whom?"[4] From whatever angle one answers these questions, the stereotype is condescending to racial minorities because it implies that Asian Americans are remarkable when compared to other racial minorities and serve as a model for other people of color to emulate.

2. Kang, "Korean Americans Dream of Crimson."

3. Daniel A. Bell describes the rise of Asian Americans as the greatest success story in our country in "The Triumph of Asian Americans," 24.

4. Frank H. Wu, *Yellow*, 59.

The praise Asian Americans receive as the model minority is fundamentally racial, breeding resentment among those who confirm the stereotype and those who are implicitly insulted and denigrated by it.[5] The
argument for those who support the model minority goes something like
this: if Asian Americans can succeed despite discrimination and racism
through hard work, grit, and determination, then why can't blacks? The
American racial landscape is certainly more diverse than white, Asian
American, and black. However, as Claire Jean Kim explains, the praise of
Asian American cultural values "has always worked in tandem with explicit constructions of blacks as culturally deficient."[6] While this ideology
does not deny the existence of discrimination and racism against Asian
Americans, blacks, Latino/as, and other racial-ethnic minoritized groups,
it diverts attention away from the systemic problems of racial discrimination and the importance of leveling the playing field for *all* racial-ethnic
minorities.[7] It inherently pits Asian Americans against other people of
color by valorizing us relative to whites, who continue to be the standard-
bearers for mainstream success.

The greatest damage of the model minority myth is that it perpetuates
the notion that racial barriers can be overcome through good behaviors,
implying that if other people of color (namely blacks) behaved better, they
too would overcome inequality and racism.[8] The myth falsely perpetuates
that Asian Americans have managed to achieve socioeconomic success in
the face of racial and economic inequity by pulling themselves up by their
own bootstraps without the help of government aid or need to speak out
and protest against structural and institutional racism. It fails to recognize

5. Take as a case in point the provocative headline, "Why Chinese Mothers Are Superior," given to an excerpt of Chua's book printed by the *Wall Street Journal*. This double-
edged compliment intentionally plays into the anxiety and insecurity white American
parents feel about their own parenting style.

6. Claire J. Kim, "Racial Triangulation," 118, 121. We find this explicit argument that
praises Asian Americans in contrast to blacks based on cultural grounds in Petersen's
"Success Story, Japanese-American Style."

7. Stacey J. Lee, *Unraveling the Model Minority Stereotype*. To better understand the
model minority stereotype, we must consider the ways that government, social, and
economic policies have employed various strategies to prevent blacks, Latino/as, Native
Americans, and Asian Americans from having access to the same opportunities as white
Americans.

8. The idea that there are "good" minorities and "bad" minorities works in tandem
with the narrative of American exceptionalism, which casts the US as the "model nation"
that defends freedom and democracy not only for Americans but for all free nations.

the advantageous educational backgrounds some Asian immigrants had before coming to the US. It also disregards the socioeconomic disadvantages of other Asian immigrants.

The Asian Americans who have attained educational success have not done so exclusively because they possess the "right" cultural values or traits, such as a grittier work ethic and stronger family values. Important structural and institutional factors have also played critical roles in the educational attainment of the children of Asian immigrants. In particular, the Immigration and Nationality Act of 1965 gave preference to a stream of highly-educated and skilled Asian immigrants who came from diverse socioeconomic backgrounds and with a broad range of skills. Thus, the starting point for many of these "hyper-selected" Asian immigrants put their children at greater educational advantage than the children of other Asian immigrant groups, such as Cambodians, Laotians, and Hmong.[9]

While Asian Americans comprise a very diverse group, the model minority stereotype falsely depicts us as a well-educated, prosperous, self-reliant, and quiescent monolith. Contrary to the model minority myth, hard work, strong cultural values, and education are not enough to succeed. Despite the fact that Asian Americans are statistically overrepresented at elite colleges and universities, Asian American representation at those schools as a whole has not increased over the past three decades.[10] Furthermore, Asian Americans are vastly underrepresented in upper management and executive-level positions,[11] suggesting the existence of a "bamboo ceiling" that Wesley Yang incisively describes as "an invisible barrier that maintains a pyramidal racial structure throughout corporate America, with lots of Asians at junior levels, quite a few in middle management, and virtually none in the higher reaches of leadership."[12]

When the supposed model minority takes on majority status, whites become less enthralled with the successes and values of Asian Americans. In her 2005 report on the "The New White Flight" taking place in two high-performing high schools in Silicon Valley, Suein Hwang explains that many negative raced-based presumptions are involved in the white exodus in this area.[13] White families find the high schools in this area increasingly

9. Jennifer Lee and Zhou, *The Asian American Paradox.*

10. Musto, "Does the Ivy League Discriminate?"

11. Gee et al., *Hidden in Plain Sight.*

12. Yang, "Paper Tigers." See Hyun, *Breaking the Bamboo Ceiling.*

13. Hwang, "The New White Flight."

unappealing because they are becoming "too competitive" and "too Asian." Meanwhile, in a high school in Palo Alto (a city near Silicon Valley) where white students still outnumber their Asian American counterparts and where the academic rigor, course load, homework, and competition remain very high, we do not see a growing number of white students leaving for less competitive institutions. This has led some Asian families to suggest, "It's not academic competition that makes white parents uncomfortable but academic competition with Asian-Americans."[14] So long as Asian Americans do not pose a threat to whites, they are a model minority. However, when they "take up" spots in colleges or the job market that white students desire, they lose their status as "honorary whites" and become "perpetual foreigners"[15] who "take over" schools, communities, and institutions.

I went to UCLA for college, an institution that has been unofficially coined the "University of Caucasians Lost among Asians." I have heard this joke for years from the mouths of white and Asian American students alike, but it has continued to frustrate and offend me for a number of reasons. First of all, the acronym smacks of insidious racism and unresolved fears. It conveys the idea that Asians or Asian Americans are somehow taking over UCLA's campus, leaving white students at risk of becoming invisible, displaced minorities, who are somehow "lost" among a collective mass of ubiquitous, indistinguishable black-haired, yellow-toned, slanted-eye students. If the school's undergraduate student body were not made up of 28.6 percent Asian (in contrast to 27 percent of whites) but remained the predominantly white school that it once was before the 1990s, I highly doubt that people would joke that the undergraduate student body is overrepresented and overrun by white students.[16] Secondly, the acronym makes whites out to be the norm. Asians serve as dominant backdrop to white students, who serve as the school's central cast of characters. Lastly,

14. Hwang, "The New White Flight."

15. The image of the "perpetual foreigner" has also been a prevailing narrative burdening Asian Americans, one that even their "model minority" status cannot seem to mitigate. They are interconnected representations that play off each other and place Asian Americans in vulnerable racial positions (Ng et al., "Contesting," 96). See, e.g., Wan, "Asian American Perspectives," 175–90; Yee, "She Stood in Tears," 119–40; and Tuan, *Forever Foreigners or Honorary Whites?*

16. Figures from "UCLA Profile, Fall 2016" found at http://www.aim.ucla.edu/profiles2.aspx.

it disregards the students belonging to other racial-ethnic groups, as if the only racial minorities that matter are those of Asian descent.[17]

The 1992 LA Riots serve as an example of how that the status of the model minority is precarious and can quickly turn negative depending on the political interest of the dominant group in power. The riots show how the white media uses the model minority myth as a double-edged sword against other minoritized groups. As soon as the riots erupted, the mainstream media exploited the downside of the model minority myth for the protection of white interest by quickly turning Korean Americans into callous, un-American, selfish, ethnocentric people—debasing their virtue of hard work into greed, and their strong family values into ethnocentrism. The tragic incident shows that there is only a nominal difference in the white imagination of Korean Americans: they are either exceptional immigrants (the model minority) or they are heartless foreigners or even racists.[18]

CONTESTING THE MODEL MINORITY STEREOTYPE

Being Asian American involves negotiating contradictions, multiple belongings, particularities, intergenerational conflict and consensus, and existential conflict and consensus. As Asian Americans Christians, many of us still struggle to live a coherent life among the many incoherent or contradictory narratives of the dominant culture, within our minoritized cultures, within the hearts and minds of our parents, and within our own hearts and minds. Most of us will grapple with how to integrate our cultural, racial-ethnic, social, civic, and Christian identities, so that we are not so compartmentalized in how we understand ourselves. We will continue to hold in tension the complexities that come with belonging and never quite belonging to American society as Asian Americans Christians. But there are some actions we can take to begin to disrupt the problematic assumptions and ramifications of being socially inscribed as the model minority.

First, we must be critical of the double-edged nature of the model minority narrative, while acknowledging the ways it has advantageously served us. Being stereotyped as smart, hardworking, and high-achieving has benefited some Asian American students because they are more likely

17. According to the same figures ("UCLA Profile"), Hispanic/Latino students make up 21.7 percent of UCLA's 2016 undergraduate student body.

18. I am grateful to Hak Joon Lee for this insight.

to be put on a more competitive academic track and achieve at higher levels by way of self-fulfilling prophecy.[19] That said, those who do not live up to this expectation feel like failures, outliers, and a discredit to their race. The flip side to the smart, hardworking stereotype of Asian Americans becomes especially prominent in the workplace, as Asian Americans are perceived as being peacemakers, averse to risk, and lacking in leadership qualities and soft skills. Studies show Asian Americans who break this cultural stereotype by being assertive and dominant are not only less liked by their coworkers but also receive more harassment than those Asian Americans who do not.[20] As long as we remain in relatively subordinate positions to whites, we pose a minimum threat to them and are more likely to be lauded as model minorities.[21] However, when we behave assertively and take on higher positions of leadership, we pose both economic and social threats to whites[22] and are more likely to be stigmatized as a despised minority.[23]

Second, when we recognize that we have historically and personally experienced inequality, prejudice, racism, and exclusion as Asian Americans, we can be less naïve about a romantic "Asian American success story" that posits us as honorary whites and much better than other racial-ethnic cultures. When we buy into the narrative that we Asian Americans are hardworking, polite, deferential, peaceable, and quiet in contrast to other people of color, we end up alienating ourselves from other minoritized populations and becoming allies with those who seek to protect white privilege.

19. Thomsen, "The Asian American Achievement Paradox."

20. Berdahl and Min, "Prescriptive Stereotypes and Workplace Consequences," 141–52.

21. Berdahl and Min, "Prescriptive Stereotypes and Workplace Consequences," 142–43."

22. Berdahl and Min, "Prescriptive Stereotypes and Workplace Consequences," 142.

23. Prior to being valorized as the model minority, Asian Americans were stigmatized and otherized as the problematic Oriental (Yu, *Thinking Orientals*, 7). American history is fraught with conceptions of Asians/Asian Americans as foreign and dangerous enemies. The Chinese Exclusion Act of 1882 excluded Chinese immigrant laborers from the country based on the argument that they came from a "degraded and inferior race" and claims that "Oriental civilization" was incompatible with American culture and an economic threat to American labor (Erika Lee, *The Making of Asian America*, 89). The xenophobic, psycho-cultural fear of colored people from the East, known as the "Yellow Peril," resulted from American involvement in wars in Japan, Korea, and Viet Nam. During World War II, 120,000 Japanese Americans (two-thirds of them US citizens) were forcibly removed from their homes and communities in the West Coast and incarcerated in "internment camps" for the crime of being of Japanese descent and in the name of homeland security (Lee, *The Making*, 212).

Third, we need to recognize and be in solidarity with other Asian American communities of South East Asian and South Asian descent, who are often disregarded and hurt most by the implications of the model minority myth. South East Asian Americans, particularly Cambodians, Laotians, and Hmong, are often swept up and cast aside by the model minority myth even as they have poverty rates similar to blacks, Latino/as, and Natives.[24] South Asians, particularly those who are Muslims or Sikhs, struggle against the terrorist stereotype in the post 9/11 and 11/9 era. This is why Ellen Wu underscores how the model minority tells only part of the story of Asian American life.[25] Although the stereotypes of the model minority and the terrorist differ significantly, they are nevertheless related because they speak to the broader political anxieties of their times.[26]

REVISITING A PERILOUS SUCCESS STORY

In the book of Esther, we have a protagonist with serious social disadvantages. Esther is a female, orphan, diaspora Jew living in the Persian empire. This makes her not only member of a marginalized group of immigrants, but also a particularly vulnerable member within her already vulnerable community. Esther also has some significant social advantages. She is extraordinarily beautiful and was brought up like a daughter by her cousin, Mordecai. Although Mordecai is not part of King Ahasuerus's inner court, he is "in the know" about the important conversations taking place inside and outside of the palace walls.[27] Mordecai is a model minority who protects Persian privilege when he literally saves the king from an assassination plot conspired against him (2:21–23). Mordecai is also a perpetual foreigner. Even though he saves the king's life, he becomes a victim of racism and prejudice when he refuses to pay obeisance to Haman, the king's newly promoted official. Infuriated, Haman comes up with a plot to not only kill Mordecai but to "destroy all the Jews" (3:6).

Just as Haman's antagonism for one incompliant and disobedient Jew results in a legal decree to annihilate all Jews, so the king's anger against the incompliant and disobedient Queen Vashti results in a law requiring all women to honor their husbands (1:20). Such discriminatory laws reflect

24. Bruenig, "Asian Poverty and the 'Model Minority.'"

25. See Ellen D. Wu, *The Color of Success*.

26. Guo, "The Real Reasons the U.S. Became Less Racist Toward Asian Americans."

27. Fox, *Character and Ideology in the Book of Esther*, 57.

the (il)logic of stereotypes, misogyny, and racism and serve as a warning to other would-be intractable women and Jews. Unlike the bold and brazen Vashti, Esther makes use of what John C. Scott calls "the weapons of the weak" and the hidden "arts of resistance" through her behind-the-scenes strategizing.[28] Rather than go before the king to boldly petition him to save her people from genocide, she disarms and charms him with a dinner invitation. She has the ability and resources to prepare sumptuous meals, so she uses food and feasting to curry the favor of the king on behalf of her people. Although Esther does not appear to exhibit the characteristics and actions of an outspoken and assertive hero, she makes use of her partial privilege as the queen of the Persian king and her partial oppression as his subordinated wife to advocate on behalf of her despised people and prevent their genocide.

When first warned of Haman's plan to annihilate all Jews, Esther feels powerless and understandably self-preserving. Mordecai implores her to go before the king to intercede on behalf of her people. At first she declines, citing the law that anyone who goes to the king's inner court without being invited shall be put to death. By advocating and intervening for her people, she would be subjecting herself to grave danger. The fact that prior to this Mordecai has commanded her to keep her ethnic identity a secret (2:10) suggests that he sensed or knew from experience that there are advantages and privileges associated with being non-Jewish in Persia and potential disadvantages and perils associated with being Jewish.[29] Thus, Esther faces "overlapping risks in approaching the king—she has not been invited and she might be found out to be a Jew, both of which, in this case, mean death."[30]

After being "woke" by Mordecai (4:13–14), Esther seizes the opportunity to speak up and use her identity as a woman loved by the king to save her fellow Jews who were loathed by Haman. She disrupts the triangulation between the Jews, the king, and the rest of the king's subjects by advocating as a Jew who is intimately familiar to the king for Jews whom the king perceives as "others." In doing so, she helps challenge the negative stereotypes made against her people and allays some of the animosity harbored against them. She effects legislative change by negotiating the deal that revoked the official decree against her people and consequently empowers them to

---

28. See Scott, *Weapons of the Weak* and *Domination and the Arts of Resistance*.

29. Anderson, *Ancient Laws*, 68.

30. Halvorson-Taylor, "Secrets and Lies," 481.

maintain their language and writings and defend themselves against those who wished to annihilate them (8:5–14). She also coauthors an edict authorizing the observance of a Jewish religious festival in the land of Persia (9:29). As Nikki Toyama-Szeto points out, "Esther goes from being a vulnerable minority woman to an advocate and policy-maker in the Persian Empire."[31] And though it was not required socially and politically for Esther to take on this new status as law shaper and lawmaker, she makes use of her privileged position to help bring attention to the perils facing and issues concerning her people.

Esther does not see herself as someone who can change the fate of her people. What could she do on behalf of her fellow Jews in her position of partial and precarious privilege and limited access to power? Mordecai, however, reminds Esther of the risk she takes by not doing anything: "Do not think that in the king's palace you will escape any more than all the other Jews. For if you keep silent at such a time as this, relief and deliverance will rise for the Jews from another quarter, but you and your father's family will perish" (4:13–14). In other words, "Esther, don't think your high and hidden position will keep you safe. Today you may be favored but tomorrow you may be hated. If you act, God can use you. If you don't, God will still save his people. But you have a chance to be a part of God's divine intentions." Once Esther grasps the gravity of the situation and the opportunity, she changes. She sees differently. She acts strategically and with agency and purpose. She speaks out. She takes great risks.

Esther's circumstances are certainly not to be admired or romanticized, and her approach to effecting change can be criticized. However, Esther serves as a biblical example of a diaspora minority who balances competing obligations to her family and her fellow Jews with survival in a Gentile world.[32] She also succeeds in attaining structural power and societal influence by using her resources and privileges to secure the well-being of her people. Like Esther, we must learn how to use our privileges as the favored (and in her case hidden) minority not to protect and perpetuate our precarious and problematic position as the model minority, but rather to advocate for Asian Americans. We must, however, do more than advocate for ourselves. We need to stand in solidarity with other people of color—many of whom have gone before us in fighting for civil rights and

31. Toyama, "Getting Used to the Sound of My Voice," 170.
32. Halvorson-Taylor, "Secrets and Lies," 485.

racial justice and equality—by advocating for their equal treatment as well as ours and supporting that their lives indeed matter.

Esther is a person who has built and expanded her power base for her own people while working within a Persian-controlled system. How can we build and expand our power base as Asian Americans while working in white-controlled institutions? How can we work strategically and collaboratively against rather than be in passive collusion with stereotypes, systems, and laws that disadvantage and endanger others? Like Mordecai, how can we be exilic outsiders in the sense that we are willing to shatter the image of the model minority by refusing to accept systems and laws that unjustly value some lives over others or discriminate against others?

REFRAMING SUCCESS AND WHAT IT MEANS TO BE EXCEPTIONAL

A challenge we face as Asian American Christians is recognizing that our identity as exceptional does not come from our supposed genetic academic superiority or from meeting the certain expectations and stereotypes that we are all supposed to be straight-A students, born and bred for certain types of careers. Our exceptional status—and this is true for Christians of every race and ethnicity—is in our identity in Christ. That said, debunking the model minority stereotype does not do away with our unique differences and contributions. There are many ways of being Asian American, just as there are many expressions of being Christian. But we need to learn to live as people formed into the image of Christ, rather than as people formed in the image of the model minority stereotype that makes us out to be "good" and others out to be "bad."

We can resist being pitted against blacks, Latino/as, and other racial-ethnic groups by forging alliances and working in solidarity with them in their political activism and struggle for civil rights and equity. Some ways we can challenge the myth of the model minority is by speaking out against it, refusing to be a silent privileged minority, and increasing our civic engagement and political participation to advocate for ourselves and other racial-ethnic minority groups that face discrimination. We can use our partial privilege *and* partial oppression to critique systems of oppression and inequality, to welcome refugees coming to our shores from Syria and other war-torn countries, advocating for their sanctuary, safety, housing, healthcare, and to denounce rhetorics of exclusion and narratives of demonization whenever and wherever they arise.

There is a tendency among Asian Americans to want to identify with whites more than blacks or other people of color, since being accepted as "honorary whites"[33] seems like the formula for assimilation and upward mobility.[34] Buying into the myth of the model minority distances us from "the other" when we hear of a Muslim ban or the building a wall between the US and Mexico or see protests supporting Black Lives Matter. Quietly accepting rather than loudly contesting the model minority myth causes us to identify more with privileged members of the dominant culture rather than the less privileged members of our own ascribed communities.[35] The myth of the model minority pits us against the very people we must struggle with for racial equality in our nation. It also reinscribes the false notion that by gaining entry into our nation's most prestigious institutions and/or attaining financial success, we will be protected from racial discrimination and spared from being perceived as perpetual foreigners. The tragic murder of Vincent Chin in 1982 soberly reminds us that this is not the case. The model minority stereotype has done little to actually change the widely held perception that Asian Americans are not "real" Americans.[36]

Although stories of Asian American success receive the most attention by Asian Americans and the dominant culture alike, what about our stories of the seemingly less successful? What theological significance do they have for us? How can Asian Americans succeed in life while failing to fit into the narrative of the model minority? Many of our parents have sacrificed their dreams so that we can achieve our own. Rather than dream for ourselves alone, how can our dreams of justice contest the model minority stereotype and white supremacy? How can we partner with those seeking to do similar work out of our love for God and the desire for equal rights and justice for all? How can we occupy a new space, not as a proxy for whites or relative to blacks, Latino/as, and other communities of color, but as Asian American Christians who creatively and collectively use our faith, voices, cultures, upbringings, educational and socioeconomic backgrounds, experiences,

33. See Claire J. Kim, "Asian Americans Are People of Color, Too . . . Aren't They?," 30.

34. Frank H. Wu, "How do Asian Americans Advocate for Equality?"

35. Frank H. Wu, "How do Asian Americans Advocate for Equality?"

36. See, e.g., Luo, "An Open Letter to the Woman Who Told My Family to Go Back to China," *New York Times* (Oct 9, 2016), https://www.nytimes.com/2016/10/10/nyre-gion/to-the-woman-who-told-my-family-to-go-back-to-china.html.

disadvantages, and privileges to promote the flourishing of those around us?

DISCUSSION QUESTIONS:

1. In what ways have you silently bought into the myth of the model minority? In what ways have you contested it?

2. How does the stereotype of the model minority affect your relationship with your parents, whites, and other people of color? How does it affect your self-esteem?

3. How has the notion of being a "good" minority shaped your idea of being a "good" Christian and vice-versa?

4. How would you (re)define "success" for yourself as an Asian American Christian? How might your understanding of being successful go against the societal, cultural, and religious expectations to be polite, work hard without complaining, live quietly, and avoid rocking the boat?

10

COMMUNITY

HAK JOON LEE

Beverly Tatum, a famous African American psychologist and the president of Spelman College, wrote a book with a provocative title *Why Are All The Black Kids Sitting Together in the Cafeteria?*[1] Her book analyzes the phenomenon of African American students sitting, eating, and talking together in high school and college cafeterias. Why do they do that? At those tables, they can be themselves without wearing a social mask and freely talk about all issues affecting their personal and social lives, including race, food, music, and spirituality. According to Tatum, the phenomenon has to do with the development of racial identity—an acute and active search for one's racial identity that takes place in the late teens and the early twenties.[2] As they grow up, African Americans begin to recognize race as an integral part of their identity. They actively look for the spaces that offer social and emotional support as well as information on social networks and cultural resources unique to their community.[3]

Interestingly, Tatum's observation applies to Asian Americans as well. Indeed, many Asian American kids choose to sit together in cafeterias, and this same social-psychological dynamic drives Asian Americans to Asian American churches (or English Ministry congregations) during or after

1. Tatum, *Why Are All The Black Kids Sitting Together in the Cafeteria?*
2. Tatum, *Why Are All The Black Kids Sitting Together in the Cafeteria?*, 52.
3. Tatum, *Why Are All The Black Kids Sitting Together in the Cafeteria?*, 59–62.

college. Their journey starts as early as middle or high school, typically in a cafeteria, and continues to college, later extending to churches after they graduate.

When I was a student in seminary there were two major self-segregated tables: one for African Americans, the other for Asian Americans. Whites could go to any table they chose, but they would go mostly to tables with other whites. Every on-campus residential member of the seminary knew it. I remember holding a food tray in my hand and looking for a table where other Asian Americans were sitting. White students would often ask me why Asian Americans were so clannish, gathering just among themselves rather than mingling with people of other races. This question was usually sharper and more pointed among evangelical students. Many of them had difficulty accepting this de facto, self-imposed racial segregation among people of color. Their message was: we are all Christians, and there should be no division; separate tables do not contribute to the unity of Christians in Jesus Christ, and Asian Americans are obviously failing to live up to this charge of the gospel.

So, why are many Asian American students flocking together in the cafeteria even though they speak accent-free English? The Asian American search for a community to call their own has to do with a basic human need for emotional and social support. Humans are social beings inextricably related to others. Every human being has a deep thirst for authentic community where one is accepted and cared for, and where one can actualize oneself. Scripture also acknowledges the interdependent nature of human life. For example, in Genesis 2 God said, "It is not good for the man to be alone. I will make a helper suitable for him." When Asian Americans are lonely, isolated, or marginalized (meaning they do not receive institutional support), they feel powerless; they are afraid of sharing their deep feelings and emotions. However, when they can express themselves—their anxiety, fear, desire, pain, and hope—then they feel empowered. The significance of a community for human development and thriving cannot be overemphasized. Philip Selznick notes:

> Without supportive contexts of nurture and sustenance, and of inspiration as well, selfhood is at risk. When continuities of practice and judgments are discounted or abandoned people become footloose, reactive . . . . To be truly independent, self-confident, and resourceful people need foundations.[4]

4. Selznick, *The Moral Commonwealth*, 12.

Ongoing social fragmentation in a globalizing society further compels Asian Americans to seek a community among their Asian American friends and communities.

The cafeteria table has to do with unique social-psychological dynamics that people experience in a racialized society. The self-segregated tables in a school cafeteria reflect the reality of the race relationships in US society. Like African Americans, Asian Americans feel a strong need for their own social spaces. Asian Americans, though they were born (or at least grew up) in the US, feel unfit or marginalized by the various ways society presents cultural symbols, portrays body images, and enforces social expectations. Out of cultural confusion and emotional dissonance, they naturally turn to those who not only understand them but also share the same struggles. As part of the search for their identity, young Asian Americans almost intuitively realize that their personal identity is incomplete without a positive affirmation of their racial identity and celebration of their racial and ethnic heritages. They seek their own social space where they can be free, where all can express their candid feelings, culturally sensitive issues, or practice their cultural habits that a dominant society neither understands nor is interested in. The table at the cafeteria offers Asian Americans the space where they find much needed personal support and cultural affirmation to explore authentic selfhood.

ASIAN AMERICAN SEARCH FOR COMMUNITY

However, a racialized relationship in society is not the only force that pushes Asian Americans to herd together. In addition to racial alienation in mainstream institutions, there is another social force that drives Asian Americans to Asian American churches: they do not feel at home in Asian immigrant churches. Though improving, many Asian immigrant churches still remain quite authoritarian and traditional in their understanding of sex roles in their culture and ethos. Young Asian Americans feel that their voices are not heard there. Communication is often one-sided rather than mutual. They begin to notice that the church is the extension of traditional patriarchal Asian families. Often treated as junior or inexperienced, young Asian Americans find themselves on the receiving end of the commands. In particular, Asian American women feel they are treated as inferior to men; they are expected to be passive and compliant rather than independent and assertive. One cannot ignore the significant differences between the two generations in terms of theological perspectives, cultural experiences, and moral orientations. For example, while the first-generation immigrant Christians are generally disapproving of prevalent social issues such as alcohol consumption, sex, and homosexuality, the EM (English Ministry) is more likely to be tolerant or even accepting.[5]

Young Asian Americans do not find much of a home at Asian immigrant churches, and are leaving in large numbers—more women than men—in search of their own "promised land."[6] Whenever opportunity knocks, they create their own segregated space within immigrant churches or move from immigrant churches, flocking to Asian American churches or starting a completely new church.

Asian Americans feel that they are disconnected from mainstream society and disempowered by Asian immigrant churches. Young Asian Americans struggle to put their world in order, but without much help from either culture—one eager but incompetent (family and immigrant churches), the other neither competent nor eager (mainstream society). Where do they find resources for personal support and strengths? They look for a community where they can be themselves without fear, whether it is a segregated table in the cafeteria, an Asian American church, or a circle of friends.

Despite their good intentions and ardent search for a community, however, many Asian Americans find that it is not easy to build a good community. Good intentions run into unexpected challenges and end in disappointment. They find that they are unprepared for the task; they do not know what constitutes a "good" community nor how to build it. This limitation comes partly from their experience of growing up in families and communities that discourage genuine open conversations and egalitarian relationships, and partly because of the highly mobile, contractual, anonymous nature of US social life. That is, as US society gets more fragmented, it is difficult to find a lasting committed relationship or a place where one can experience a good community.

5. Johnny Lee, "No Such Thing . . . " 231.

6. This is often referred to as "the silent exodus."

HOW TO BUILD A COMMUNITY: BEYOND INDIVIDUALISM AND COLLECTIVISM

Asian Americans face two harmful kinds of relationships in contemporary society: individualistic contractual relationships that are prevalent in a postmodern culture, or authoritarian relationships that are prevalent in Asian immigrant communities.[7] A contractual relationship affirms our freedom, but does not meet our need for intimacy and belonging, while a collectivistic community may offer a sense of security but does not respect individual freedom and creativity. However, freedom and security are not things that we should have to choose between. We long for freedom and independence as much as we want enduring friendship and acceptance in a community. Our experience tells us that humans are both relational and reflective. Freedom and security—the two contrasting desires—are in permanent tension in a human life. If we choose freedom over security, then we feel lonely. However, when we choose security over freedom, we are afraid of losing our independence.

A THIRD WAY: COVENANT

How can we reconcile freedom and security? What does Scripture say about this dilemma? What is the biblical idea of a good community, and how can we build such a community?

At the center of a biblical idea of a community is covenant, which forms the structure and dynamic process of a community. Unlike other relationships (or transactions), covenant is based on trust. To put it simply, covenant refers to a sustained entrusted relationship under the supervision of God. It is established upon trust through the exchange of a promise (a pledge or oath) by the participants with God as the guarantor of the pledged commitment.[8] Unlike a contract, because of God's supervision, the pledges made in covenant are solemn and the accountability in relationship goes beyond immediate human partners.

I believe that trust is the answer to this dilemma between individualism and collectivism that many young Asian Americans struggle with in

7. Metaphorically speaking, these two choices are similar to either being grains of sand (relationship without cohesion and bond), or drops of water in the ocean (relationship without individuality).

8. Allen, *Love and Conflict*.

their lives. Trust is the solution because it offers a secure and firm relationship that is also open and respectful of our individuality. Trust is the fiber and glue of a relationship. Trust, in its ordinary sense, pertains to the belief in the integrity and reliability of a person. Trust is an interpersonal dynamic that reconciles freedom with security. How is it possible? First, trust is an act of freedom. No one can be forced to trust. Trust is a free decision made on the basis of plausible reason or warrant. Trust is also the basis of security. Once trust is established, we are willing to take risks beyond our immediate self-interest. Trust serves as the basis for further committed (thus risk-involving) interactions. When there is trust, we take the risk of vulnerability by opening ourselves toward others. Only when we feel trusted and trusting are we more confident in sharing our deepest thoughts, honest opinions, or constructive criticisms. Without trust, a long-term healthy relationship is unthinkable.

Trust is the basis of a community. Without a healthy relationship, there can be no healthy community, and the community built upon trust is neither contractual (individualistic) nor hierarchical; it is reciprocal and egalitarian.[9]

For Christians, this trust is primarily learned from our covenantal relationship with God. God first loved us, and our trust is a response to God's initiating love. A Christian community is built upon our response to this faithfulness of God toward humanity in Jesus Christ. Our relationship with others is the outworking of divine covenant. Our spiritual life begins with our response to God's amazing, unconditional love demonstrated in the life, death, and resurrection of Jesus Christ. The church is the community that is built upon those who trust in God's faithfulness; this trusting relationship with God is so deep and thick, the Apostle Paul describes it using the phrase "union with Christ." Indeed, our relationship with God and others stands and falls with trust, and thus we are called to hold onto faith in God and build trust with each other.

With mutual trust as its foundation, covenant goes a step further by bringing the parties into even deeper commitment toward each other. A covenant institutionalizes trust into a particular form of enduring relationship. That is, on the basis of entrusted relationship, a covenant develops mutual agreement that outlines the responsibility of each participant. The

---

9. Therefore, trust is a precondition for love; genuine love grows out of mutual trust.

mutual agreement has the effect of binding the participants into a shared goal and a certain course of actions.

Second, a good community is built upon justice (righteousness). A covenant relationship is guided by God's moral laws (such as the Ten Commandments) that reflect God's moral character. A covenant is technically different from a contract; the latter is motivated by self-interest (specified by mutual legal obligation) while covenant is moral in nature (which goes beyond legal obligations). To establish a strong covenant, participants need to find a common moral cause or shared values to which they willingly commit, and then develop a common action plan (in the form of agreement) that delineates mutual responsibility among the participants. For Christians, the content of the covenant—in particular, the agreed-upon terms—should accord with God's will.

Millennials tend to show suspicion toward the law or moral codes. However, relationship without shared norms and values is unstable and unpredictable; norms and values help protect each party from abuse, and add stability to relationships. A covenantal community is not just the gathering of like-minded people for the sake of personal comfort, emotional needs, or shared hobbies. Although affection or good intention is important, neither alone is sufficient. Our relationship is more enduring when it is mediated by mutually shared moral values (integrity, fairness, care, forgiveness). Shared values (which are codified into the agreed-upon terms in covenant) serve as the criteria of adjudication as well as the basis of commitment. Shared values are important because they sustain the relationship long-term. To enter a covenant relationship is to voluntarily commit oneself to the other party; shared agreement reminds the participants of a common cause that coheres with or serves God's design and will for that particular relationship (as the parties establish). Relationships that are not based on shared values do not last long, because they are based on emotion or self-interest.[10] Core moral values and convictions offer the shared standards of actions that help to coordinate mutual expectations and interactions among the members. In other words, covenant has the effect of turning people into moral agents. Because of this intrinsic nature of justice, covenant is not purely private; it has public meaning as well. It is an agreement *before* God. God is the

---

10. A common misunderstanding in postmodern society is that a community is made of an emotional attachment among like-minded people. Emotional attachment is important, but without shared values it cannot last long since emotions are fleeting and ephemeral.

overseer of the covenant. Furthermore, covenant is missionally oriented. *It serves God's purpose: the flourishing of all lives.*

In addition to shared values, a covenantal relationship requires certain practices to keep it alive and fulfill its goal. A good community is not given, but built among us through a long, patient process of cultivating trust between the members through ongoing exchanges of affection, goods, and ideas. It is like hand-weaving a fabric with yarn by laying and intertwining fibers one by one. Building trust requires patience, mutual investment of time and energy, care, acceptance, forgiveness, and commitment to shared values. It also requires frequent and honest communication and interactions of sharing stories, pains, joys, and hopes. A covenantal relationship does not require our perfection; it requires honesty, transparency, and timely communication.

BIBLICAL AND THEOLOGICAL RESPONSES

The story of Daniel and his three friends offers good insight for Asian Americans by illuminating the psychosocial dynamics of the Asian American search for community. The book of Daniel begins with the story of four young friends—Daniel, Hananiah, Mishael, and Azariah—who were brought to Babylon as captives. One could easily imagine the kind of trauma these four men underwent. They were forcibly separated from their homeland, temple, and their parents and siblings; they were members of an ethnic minority in captivity within the powerful empire; they had no available mentors or religious and community leaders around them; they were completely by themselves without protection or any hope of returning home. Additionally, there was the enormous pressure to assimilate, which is evidenced by their forced adoption of new Babylonian names: "The chief official gave them new names: to Daniel, the name Belteshazzar; to Hananiah, Shadrach; to Mishael, Meshach; and to Azariah, Abednego" (Dan 1:7). Refusal to assimilate or obey could lead to expulsion from the court or severe punishment. They were powerless no matter how smart and intelligent they were (Dan 1:4). By any standard, their situation appeared hopeless. They were doomed, and sheer survival could be the only reasonable goal for them.

How did Daniel and his friends respond to their predicament? They first gathered among themselves away from the Babylonians (as Asian Americans do today). It is not difficult to understand why they did this: to share the horrible experience of captivity, the loneliness of exile, and the anxiety of an unknown future, and to seek emotional support. However, what is noticeable is that their gathering did not end with mutual emotional support—venting of anxiety or lamenting. They found a common ground in their faith. They went a step further. Together they chose a shared plan of action. That is, they *covenanted* among themselves not to defile themselves with the wine and food of the king. Trust in God is not mentioned, but we can easily imagine that it is implied in the story because the narrative reveals that God blessed them with favor from the eunuch and the King, together with wisdom and knowledge.

Daniel and his friends realized that they had to be deliberate and purposeful to remain people of faith. Though limited, controlling their diet was their way of keeping their identity and asserting their moral agency in a suppressive environment. Eating and sharing food is central to one's cultural identity; it is a daily practice that profoundly shapes one's sense of self. In their situation, the control of diet was probably the only available choice they had for asserting that they were Jews no matter where they resided and whatever language they may have spoken.

Daniel and his friends' dietary practice served as the reminder of their core identity as Jews. It was a symbolically important gesture in rejecting their complete absorption into the Babylonian system. Their dietary rules helped to build a psychological boundary (an identity marker) between them and the system, and by remaining faithful they refused to exchange their dignity and identity for the material comfort and protection that the system provided.

It would not be an exaggeration to say that one's agency begins with control over one's own body, including the power to choose what goes into one's body; the control of diet means the control of agency on its most basic level. By controlling what went into their bodies, Daniel and his friends maintained some part of their freedom and control. This was a significant step on their part and, more importantly, it pleased God.

Although there were obviously other distressed Jewish captives in the king's court, Daniel's group responded to the insurmountable challenge by trusting in God and agreeing to exercise their freedom and control, no matter how small, against external pressure. By doing so, they transformed their private gathering into a moral community in God. They were willing to take a risk because they trusted God even in their besieged situation. It is safe to assume that their refusal to participate in idol worship later (Dan 3:1–16) grew out of their mutual nurturance in such a moral community.

ASIAN AMERICAN CHURCH AS GOD'S MORAL COMMUNITY

What can we learn from Daniel's story? What is a unique way Asian American Christians can develop a covenantal community that is faithful to God? Resonating with Beverly Tatum's thesis, the story of Daniel and his friends shows that humans are created to be free; they cannot be completely scripted by others.

As we saw, cultural and psychological needs drive young Asian Americans to Asian American churches. They are already involved in various practices of community life such as worship, fellowship, and small group meetings within the church where they share their personal stories and exchange prayer requests. However, in light of the covenantal principles of community forming that we discussed, their activities are somewhat limited.

If examined in light of Daniel's story, it is questionable just how much Asian Americans have turned their gathering into a moral community, and how much of the mission of Asian American churches is self-consciously concerned with social issues that affect the social well-being of all Asian Americans—their distinct social issues and struggles in our society.

In addition to seeking a space of worship, fellowship, and small groups, Asian Americans need to build a moral community in God around a higher moral cause that the members are committed to. As we discussed, the sharing of common moral causes, core moral values, and convictions is critical for community-building. And the churches need to be covenantal by consciously reaching an agreement around a shared goal and action plan as Daniel and his friends did to advance the moral cause; such a moral cause should be both expressed in the church's mission statement and translated into its practices.

Without a conscious and intentional effort to build God's covenantal community, Asian American churches may end up being a refuge for those who want to escape from the harsh realities, but who will, ironically, end up more and more assimilated into the damaging values of American culture that are competitive, hedonistic, and Eurocentric. It was the collective wisdom and decision-making of Daniel and his three friends that helped them realize the importance of resisting the enticing pressure of Babylon, even if their means of resisting were often limited and costly. The weak are usually tempted to imitate the powerful, and only conscious moral effort can resist the temptation.

The church is to be more than just a gathering of like-minded individuals. It does not exist merely to meet people's emotional and social needs; it seeks God's righteousness, justice, and love in society. In seeking God's righteousness, the church needs to teach its members to carry out God's will, especially to address social injustices. One prominent Asian American leader observes, "I've seen too many congregations that are solidly committed to right doctrine, doctrinal purity. They know all the doctrine, but it makes no difference in their practical lives."[11]

I would like to add that Asian American Christians need to be aware of the danger of living in their own subculture. While criticizing Asian immigrant churches for their clannish character, many Asian American churches are still focused primarily on internal issues, mostly concerned with meeting psychological needs or supporting individual aspirations. Under the huge influence of evangelicalism, there is also a tendency to reduce Christian faith to works of personal evangelism, identifying economic success as a sign of divine blessing, and isolating Asian American churches from their surrounding communities and the larger society. This tendency is reinforced by the pervasive individualism in US society ("What is in it for me?" "What is best for me?") that inculcates the preoccupation with having the newest fashion brands, styles, and technology while overlooking concerns for a larger moral purpose and the common good of society.[12] Consumeristic individualism all too easily cultivates passive acquiescence or indifference to social issues.

So where do Asian Americans find their moral cause? It can be several different things. However, it is clear that their moral cause should address the problems Asian Americans collectively struggle with. This means that Asian Americans need to self-consciously address issues of ethnicity, race, and cultural heritage at church—what their cultural heritage and identity mean for their faith, and vice versa. In particular, as their primary reasons to form Asian American churches is tied with their race (racialization), honest conversations on race and ethnicity from an Asian American perspective are necessary for Asian American churches to be a moral community.

11. Cha, Kang, and Lee, *Growing Healthy Asian American Churches*, 51.

12. Setran and Kiesling, *Spiritual Formation of Emerging Adulthood*, 60.

Nonetheless, Asian American churches seldom reflect theologically on issues related to their own race, ethnicity, and culture. In fact, many churches preach or teach as if they are living in a post-racial or culturally neutral society. Worship styles, messages, ethical practices, and church programs are no different from those in white evangelical churches. The messages and discourses of Asian American churches are primarily on personal relational issues and individual needs, while disregarding underlying structural dimensions and dynamics. The questions of racial justice, together with the history of social struggles and achievements of previous generations, are rarely mentioned. However, evangelical Asian American pastors need to remember that the very existence of Asian American congregations is bound up with racial and cultural concerns. Without an appreciation of their communities of origin, the history of previous generations' struggles and achievements, Asian American churches could easily turn into little more than self-pitying or self-solacing gatherings of people who feel like victims.

Asian American churches should not be a place of escape, but of reconstitution and empowerment of Asian Americans for the freedom and equality of humanity. A community is usually a place where people can write an alternative social script. When a dominant script is detrimental and demeaning to a minority group, what should the members of that group do? Left without resistance, it harms their sense of self. Humans, collectively, have the power to rescript what society has prescribed. History teaches that a minority group usually forms its own community and writes an alternative script that counters the dominant one. In US history, Jews and African Americans refused to be defined by racist and anti-Semitic scripts; they developed their own counter narratives through their religious communities.

Racial/ethnic identity is not something to be ashamed of or to suppress (as white evangelicalism teaches), nor is it something to assert to the exclusion of others (as secular liberationism teaches); it should be critically appropriated in the context of the common good of humanity. Through their collective reflection, minorities may turn their victimhood and marginalization into an opportunity to build collective moral agency that promotes human dignity, equality, and solidarity. There is nothing wrong with this self-conscious, critical embrace and celebration of one's race and ethnicity in doing church. In fact, many immigrants and religious communities in the history of the US served as a place for self-expression and the assertion of moral agency. In US history, various Christian communities offered a space to affirm racial and ethnic heritages, to meet emotional and social needs, and to nurture a healthy sense of bi-cultural identity and moral agency that is consistent with God's will. In fact, the sheer variety of Christian denominations in the US reflects the tapestry of racial and ethnic diversity of Europe. Asian Americans should not shy away from this possibility. As they gather in their own communities, they should positively but critically affirm and celebrate their cultural ethnic heritage and their core values in light of Scripture.

CONCLUSION

Everyone longs for a community in a mobile, fragmented, globalizing society. Asian Americans are no exceptions. Out of existential angst and deep social needs, Asian Americans are in search of their own space. Good company and enduring friendship is critical to social and psychological well-being. Asian American churches are the places to which young Asian Americans can flock in order to meet these needs. These churches are crucial for Asian Americans because they are one of the few places that Asian Americans can freely gather together. Asian American churches should be not only places of worship and fellowship, but also of moral community built on covenant. Asian American churches need to help build and nurture the moral agency of young Asian Americans by offering opportunities for self-determination, leadership, and critical engagement with social issues that directly affect Asian Americans. Ministry should be concrete and embodied enough to address prevalent issues of materialism, careerism, race, and gender both within and without the church. When Asian Americans engage in such ministry, they will serve God's kingdom more faithfully and effectively because their ministry is now socially concrete, historically relevant, and biblically sound as they represent a belief in and service to the God who became flesh in history.

DISCUSSION QUESTIONS:

1. Which Asian American church or Christian group do you regularly attend and why?

2. According to the chapter, how is a covenantal community different from other kinds of communities?

3. What can you learn from the story of Daniel and his friends for your own community life?

4. What can you do to turn an informal gathering or fellowship into a covenantal community? Name three things that you would do to strengthen the covenantal bond of your relationship with friends, a church cell group, or a campus Christian fellowship.

BIBLIOGRAPHY

Allen, Joseph L. *Love and Conflict: A Covenantal Model of Christian Ethics*. Lanham, MD: University Press of America, 1995.

American Psychological Association. *The Guidelines for Psychological Practice with Lesbian, Gay, and Bisexual Clients, Adopted by the APA Council of Representatives*. https://www.apa.org/pubs/journals/features/amp-a0024659.pdf.

Anderson, Cheryl B. *Ancient Laws and Contemporary Controversies: The Need for Inclusive Biblical Interpretation*. Oxford: Oxford University Press, 2009.

Arnett, Jeffrey. *Emerging Adulthood: The Winding Road from the Late Teens Through the Twenties*. Oxford: Oxford University Press, 2004.

Balswick, Judith K., and Jack O. Balswick. *Authentic Human Sexuality: An Integrated Christian Approach*. 2nd ed. Downers Grove, IL: IVP Academic, 2008.

Balthasar, Hans Urs von. *The Glory of the Lord: A Theological Aesthetics*, vol. 1, *Seeing the Form*. San Francisco: Ignatius, 1982.

Barth, Karl. *Church Dogmatics*. Vol. III, Part 4. Edinburgh: T&T Clark, 1961.

———. *Church Dogmatics*. Vol. IV, Part 1. Edinburgh: T&T Clark, 1956.

———. *Community, State and Church: Three Essays*. New York: Anchor, 1960.

Beattie, Tina. "The Theological Study of Gender." In *The Oxford Handbook of Theology, Sexuality, and Gender*, edited by Adrian Thatcher, 32–52. Oxford: Oxford University Press, 2015.

Bell, Daniel A. "The Triumph of Asian Americans: America's Greatest Success Story." *New Republic*, July 15, 1985, 24–31.

Berdahl, Jennifer L., and Ji-A Min. "Prescriptive Stereotypes and Workplace Consequences for East Asians in North America." *Cultural Diversity and Ethnic Minority Psychology* 18, no. 2 (April 2012) 141–52.

Bonhoeffer, Dietrich. *Discipleship*. Dietrich Bonhoeffer Works, vol. 4. Minneapolis: Fortress, 2003.

Brown, Wendy. *Undoing the Demos: Neoliberalism's Stealth Revolution*. New York: Zone, 2015.

Brueggemann, Walter. "Covenanting as Human Vocation." *Interpretation* 33, no. 2 (April 1979) 115–29.

———. *The Psalms and the Life of Faith*. Minneapolis: Fortress, 1995.

Bruenig, Matt. "Asian Poverty and the 'Model Minority.'" *Jacobin*, April 17, 2017. https://www.jacobinmag.com/2017/04/sullivan-new-york-magazine-model-minority-racism/.

Buechner, Frederick. *Wishful Thinking: A Seeker's ABC*. New York: HarperOne, 1993.

BuzzFeed Media. "Children of Asian Immigrants Reveal Sacrifices Their Parents Made." YouTube video. June 16, 2015. https://youtu.be/k1lDXolzhd4.

Cahalan, Kathleen A. "Callings Over a Lifetime." In *Calling All Years Good: Christian Vocation throughout Life's Seasons*, edited by Kathleen A. Cahalan and Bonnie J. Miller-McLemore, 12–32. Grand Rapids; Eerdmans, 2017.

————. "Introduction." In *Calling All Years Good: Christian Vocation Throughout Life's Seasons*, edited by Kathleen A. Cahalan and Bonnie J. Miller-McLemore, 1–11. Grand Rapids: Eerdmans, 2017.

Calvin, John. *Institutes of Christian Religion*. Philadelphia: Westminster John Knox, 1960.

Cavanaugh, William T. *Theopolitical Imagination*. Edinburgh: T&T Clark, 2003.

Cha, Peter, Steve Kang, and Helen Lee. *Growing Healthy Asian American Churches*. Downers Grove, IL: InterVarsity, 2006.

Chang, Tai, and Christine J. Yes. "Using Online Groups to Provide Support to Asian-American Men: Racial, Cultural, Gender, and Treatment Issues." *Professional Psychology: Research and Practice* 34, no. 6 (2003) 634–43.

Chapman, Gary. *The 5 Love Languages: The Secret to Love that Lasts*. Chicago: Northfield, 1992.

Cheah, Joseph, and Grace Ji-Sun Kim. *Theological Reflections on "Gangnam Style": A Racial, Sexual, and Cultural Critique*. New York: Palgrave Macmillan, 2014.

Cheng, Patrick S. "Multiplicity and Judges 19: Constructing a Queer Asian Pacific American Biblical Hermeneutics." *Semeia* (2002) 119–33.

Cho Van Riesen, Susan. "Doctor or Lawyer?" In *Following Jesus without Dishonoring Your Parents*, edited by Jeanette Yep et al., 57–60. Downers Grove, IL: InterVarsity, 1998.

Chua, Amy. *Battle Hymn of the Tiger Mother*. New York: Penguin, 2011.

Clapp, Rodney. *Tortured Wonders: Christian Spirituality for People, Not Angels*. Grand Rapids: Brazos, 2004.

Conant, Eve. "I Am Nine Years Old: Children across the World Tell Us How Gender Affects Their Lives." *Journal of the National Geographic Society* 231, no. 1 (January 2017) 30–47.

Coulter, Leah. *Rediscovering the Power of Repentance and Forgiveness*. Atlanta: Ampelon, 2006.

Crawford, Sidnie Ann White. "Esther." In *Women's Bible Commentary*, edited by Carol A. Newsom and Sharon H. Ringe, 131–37. Expanded ed. Louisville: Westminster John Knox, 1998.

Dean, Kenda Creasy. "X-Files and Unknown Gods: The Search for Truth with Postmodern Adolescents." *American Baptist Quarterly* 19, no. 1 (2000) 3–21.

Delaney, Megan A. "Gender Identity Development." In *Counseling Women Across the Life Span: Empowerment, Advocacy, and Intervention*, edited by Jill E. Schwarz, 79–94. New York: Springer, 2017.

Duckworth, Angela. *Grit: The Power of Passion and Perseverance*. New York: Scribner, 2016.

Dunn, James D. G. "Faith, Faithfulness." In *The New Interpreter's Dictionary of the Bible*, edited by Katharine D. Sakenfield, 407–23. Nashville: Abingdon, 2007.

Eng, David L., and Shinhee Han. "A Dialogue on Racial Melancholia." In *Asian American Studies Now: A Critical Reader*, edited by Wu, Jean Yu-wen Shen, and Thomas C. Chen, 55–79. New Brunswick, NJ: Rutgers University Press, 2012.

Erikson, Erik H. *Identity and the Life Cycle*. New York: International Universities Press, 1980.

Bibliography

Forward, Susan. *Toxic Parents: Overcoming Their Hurtful Legacy and Reclaiming Your Life*. New York: Bantam, 1989.

Foster, Richard J. *Celebration of Discipline: The Path to Spiritual Growth*. San Francisco: HarperSanFrancisco, 2002.

Foster, Richard J., and James Bryan Smith. *Devotional Classics*. Rev. ed. San Francisco: HarperOne, 2005.

Fox, Michael V. *Character and Ideology in the Book of Esther*. Chicago: University of Chicago Press, 1974.

Freitas, Donna. *Sex and the Soul: Juggling Sexuality, Spirituality, Romance, and Religion on America's College Campuses*. New York: Oxford University Press, 2008.

Friedman, Edwin H. *Generation to Generation: Family Process in Church and Synagogue*. New York: Guilford, 1985.

Froehich, Karlfried. "Luther on Vocation." *Lutheran Quarterly* 13, no. 2 (1999) 195–207.

Fujino, Diane C. "Extending Exchange Theory: Effects of Ethnicity and Gender on Asian American Heterosexual Relationships." In *Dissertation Abstracts International*, 1993.

Gee, Buck, et al. *Hidden in Plain Sight: Asian American Leaders in Silicon Valley*. Report for the Ascend Foundation, May 2015.

Gergen, Kenneth J. *The Saturated Self: Dilemmas of Identity in Contemporary Life*. New York: Basic, 1991.

Grenz, Stanley. *The Social God and the Relational Self*. Louisville: Westminster John Knox, 2007.

Guder, Darrell L. *The Continuing Conversion of the Church*. Grand Rapids: Eerdmans, 2000.

———. *Missional Church: A Vision for the Sending of the Church in North America*. Grand Rapids: Eerdmans, 1998.

Guo, Jeff. "The Real Reasons the U.S. Became Less Racist Toward Asian Americans." *The Washington Post*, November 9, 2016. https://www.washingtonpost.com/news/wonk/wp/2016/11/29/the-real-reason-americans-stopped-spitting-on-asian-americans-and-started-praising-them/?utm_term=.f6e341f12fbe.

Halpern-Felsher, Bonnie L., et al. "Oral Versus Vaginal Sex among Adolescents: Perceptions, Attitudes, and Behavior." *Pediatrics* 115 (2005) 845–51.

Halvorson-Taylor, Martien A. "Secrets and Lies: Secrecy Notices (Esther 2:10, 20) and Diasporic Identity in the Book of Esther." *Journal of Biblical Literature* 131, no. 3 (2012) 467–85.

Hauerwas, Stanley, and William H. Willimon. *Resident Aliens: A Provocative Christian Assessment of Culture and Ministry for People Who Know that Something is Wrong*. Nashville: Abingdon, 1989.

Hendrix, Harville, and Helen Hunt. *Giving the Love That Heals: A Guide for Parents*. New York: Pocket, 1977.

Henig, Robin Marantz. "Rethinking Gender." *Journal of the National Geographic Society* 231, no. 1 (January 2017) 48–73.

Howe, Neil, and William Strauss. *Generations: The History of America's Future, 1584 to 2069*. New York: William Morrow, 1991.

Hui, Edwin. "Personhood and Bioethics: Chinese Perspective." In *Bioethics: Asian Perspectives: A Quest for Moral Diversity*, edited by Ren-Zong Qiu, 23–43. Dordrecht: Kluwer, 2004.

Hunt, Mary. *Fierce Tenderness: A Feminist Theology of Friendship*. New York: Crossroad, 1991.

Hurh, Won Moo, and Kwang Chung Kim. "Religious Participation of Korean Immigrants in the United States." *Journal for Scientific Study of Religion* 20 (March 1990) 19–34.

Huynh, Que-Lam, et al. "Perpetual Foreigners in One's Own Land: Potential Implications for Identity and Psychological Adjustment." *Journal of Social and Clinical Psychology* 30, no. 2 (2011) 133–62.

Hwang, Suein. "The New White Flight." *The Wall Street Journal*, November 19, 2005.

Hyun, Jane. *Breaking the Bamboo Ceiling: Career Strategies for Asians: The Essential Guide to Getting in, Moving up, and Reaching the Top.* Reprint ed. New York: HarperBusiness, 2006.

Jao, Greg. "Honor and Obey." In *Following Jesus without Dishonoring Your Parents*, edited by Jeanette Yep et al., 43–56. Downers Grove, IL: InterVarsity, 1998.

Jeung, Russell. *At Home in Exile: Finding Jesus among My Ancestors and Refugee Neighbors.* Grand Rapids: Zondervan, 2016.

———. "Second-Generation Chinese Americans: The Familism of the Nonreligious." In *Sustaining Faith Traditions: Race, Ethnicity, and Religion among the Latino and Asian American Second Generation*, edited by Carolyn Chen and Russell Jeung, 197–221. New York: New York University Press, 2012.

Johnson, Jill M. "Identity and Faith." http://www.ministrymatters.com/all/entry/5383/identity-and-faith.

Johnson, Luke Timothy. *Sharing Possessions: What Faith Demands.* 2nd ed. Grand Rapids: Eerdmans, 2011.

Jubilee Project. "Jubilee Project: The Bridge." http://nbcasianamericapresents.com/thebridge.

Kang, B. J. "Creating Stories with Gene Luen Yang." *The Asian American Voice.* Podcast audio, September 13, 2016. http://www.theasianamericanvoice.com/podcast/28.

Kang, K. Connie. "Korean Americans Dream of Crimson. The Lure of Harvard Is Irresistible to Many Immigrant Parents. Some Go to Great Lengths to Prepare Their Children for What They See as an Automatic Key to Success." *Los Angeles Times*, September 25, 1996.

Kegan, Robert. *The Evolving Self: Problem and Process in Human Development.* Cambridge, MA: Harvard University Press, 1982.

Keller, Timothy J. "A New Kind of Urban Christian." *Christianity Today* (May 1, 2006). http://www.christianitytoday.com/38276?start=3.

Keller, Timothy J., and Katherine Leary Alsdorf. *Every Good Endeavor: Connecting Your Work to God's Work.* 2nd ed. New York: Penguin, 2014.

Kim, Claire J. "Asian Americans are People of Color, Too . . . Aren't They? Cross-Racial Alliances and the Question of Asian American Political Identity." *AAPI Nexus* 2, no. 1 (Winter/Spring 2004) 19–47.

Kim, Claire J. "The Racial Triangulation of Asian Americans." *Politics and Society* 27, no. 1 (1999) 105–38.

Kim, Rebecca Y. *God's New Whiz Kids? Korean American Evangelicals on Campus.* New York: New York University Press, 2006.

Kim, Sharon. *A Faith of Our Own: Second Generation Spirituality in Korean American Churches.* New Brunswick, NJ: Rutgers University Press, 2010.

King, Martin Luther, Jr. "Address at the Thirty-Fourth Annual Convention of the National Bar Association." Speech, Milwaukee, August 20, 1959. In *the Threshold of a New Decade: January 1959–December 1960*, Vol. 5 of *The Papers of Martin Luther King, Jr.*, edited by Clayborne Carson, 264–70. Berkeley, CA: University of California Press, 2005.

Kitayama, Shinobu, and H. R. Markus. "Culture and the Self: Implications for Cognition, Emotion, and Motivation." *Psychological Review* 98, no. 2 (1991) 224–53.

Kodama, Maekawa Corinne, et al. "An Asian American Perspective on Psychological Student Development Theory." In *Working with Asian American College Students*," edited by Marylu K. Mcewen et al., 45–61. San Francisco: Jossey-Bass, 2002.

Kohlman, Marla H., et al. *Notions of Family: Intersectional Perspectives: Advances in Gender Research*. Bingley: Emerald, 2013.

Kuyper, Abraham. *Common Grace: God's Gifts for a Fallen World*. Vol 1. Translated by Nelson D. Kloosterman. Bellingham, WA: Lexham, 2016.

Laser, Julie Anne, and Nicole Nicotera. *Working with Adolescents: A Guide for Practitioners: Social Work Practice with Children and Families*. New York: Guilford, 2011.

Lee, Boyung. "Teaching Justice and Living Peace: Body, Sexuality, and Religious Education in Asian-American Communities." *Religious Education* 101, no. 3 (2006) 402–19.

Lee, Daniel D. "Cultural Archetypes for a Theology of Culture in a Global Age." *Cultural Encounters* 12, no. 1 (2016) 37–53.

Lee, Erika. *The Making of Asian America: A History*. New York: Simon & Schuster, 2015.

Lee, Insook. "Homoeroticism and Homosexuality in Korean Confucian Culture." *Sacred Spaces: The E-Journal of the American Association of Pastoral Counselors*, 8 (2016) 75–94.

Lee, Jennifer, and Min Zhou. *The Asian American Paradox*. New York: Russell Sage Foundation, 2015.

Lee, Johnny. "No Such Thing . . ." In *Balancing Two Worlds*, edited by Andrew Garrod and Robert Kilkenny, 221–41. Ithaca, NY: Cornell University Press, 2013.

Lee, Jung Young. *The Trinity in Asian Perspective*. Nashville: Abingdon, 1996.

Lee, Richard M., et al. "Coping with Intergeneration Family Conflict among Asian American College Students." *Journal of Counseling Psychology* 52 (2005) 389–99.

Lee, Sang Hyun. *From a Liminal Place: An Asian American Theology*. Minneapolis: Fortress, 2010.

Lee, Stacey J. *Unraveling the Model Minority Stereotype: Listening to Asian American Youth*. 2nd ed. New York: Teachers College Press, 2009.

Lee, Yoon-Joo. "Costly Signaling: Asian Americans and the Role of Ethnicity in the Willingness to Pay More for Socially Responsible Products." *Journal of Promotion Management* 23 (2017): 277–302. https://doi.org/110.1080/20496491.2016.1267680.

Leong, Frederick, and Erin Hardin. "Career Psychology of Asian Americans: Cultural Validity and Cultural Specificity." In *Asian American Psychology: The Science of Lives in Context*, edited by Gordon C. Nagayama Hall and Sumie Okazaki, 131–52. Washington, DC: American Psychological Association, 2002.

Lewis, C. S. *The Four Loves*. New York: Harcourt, 1960.

Lim, Steve. "Asian Parents React to I Love You." YouTube video. September 23, 2014. https://youtu.be/26en95whUAk.

Liu, Yang. *Ost Trifft West*. Mainz: Verlag Hermann Schmidt, 2007.

Longnecker, Richard N. *Galatians*. Word Biblical Commentary, edited by David Hubbard. Waco: Word, 1990.

Loyd, Deborah Koehn. *Your Vocational Credo: Practical Steps to Discover Your Unique Purpose*. Downers Grove, IL: InterVarsity Press, 2015.

Luther, Martin. *Luther's Works.* Vol. 31, *Career of the Reformers I.* Philadelphia: Fortress, 1957.

———. *Luther's Works.* Vol. 36, *Word and Sacrament II.* Minneapolis: Fortress, 1959.

Ma, Pei-Wen Winnie, et al. "Managing Family Conflict over Career Decisions: The Experience of Asian Americans." *Journal of Career Development* 41, no. 6 (2014): 487–506.

MacArthur Foundation. "Gene Luen Yang: Graphic Novelist. 2016 MacArthur Fellow." YouTube video, 3:18. https://www.youtube.com/watch?v=ObxuiNGQWG4.

May, William F. *Testing the National Covenant: Fears and Appetites in American Politics.* Washington, D.C.: Georgetown University Press, 2011.

McClendon, James Wm. *Systematic Theology.* Vol. 3. Nashville: Abingdon, 2000.

McLaughlin, Chuansheng Chen, et al. "Family, Peer, and Individual Correlates of Sexual Experience among Caucasian and Asian American Late Adolescents." *Journal of Research on Adolescence* 7, no. 1 (1997) 33–53.

Mendenhall, George, and Gary Herion. "Covenant." In *The Anchor Bible Dictionary,* edited by David Noel Freedman, 1179–1202. New York: Doubleday, 1992.

Musto, Drew. "Does the Ivy League Discriminate Against Asian American Applicants?" *The Cornell Daily Sun,* October 16, 2016.

Nadal, Kevin L., and Melissa J. H. Corpus. "'Tomboys' and 'Baklas': Experiences of Lesbian and Gay Filipino Americans." *Asian American Journal of Psychology* (2012) 166–75.

Nadeau, Randall L. *Asian Religions: A Cultural Perspective.* Chichester: Wiley-Blackwell, 2014.

Newbigin, Lesslie. *Foolishness to the Greeks: The Gospel and Western Culture.* Grand Rapids: Eerdmans, 1986.

———. *The Gospel in a Pluralist Society.* Grand Rapids: Eerdmans, 1989.

Ng, Jennifer C., et al. "Contesting the Model Minority and Perpetual Foreigner Stereotypes: A Critical Review of Literature on Asian Americans in Education." *Review of Research Education* 31 (2007) 95–130.

Niebuhr, H. Richard. *Christ and Culture.* Expanded ed. New York: Harper & Row, 2001.

The Nielsen Company. *Asian Americans: Culturally Diverse and Expanding Their Footprint.* 2016. http://www.nielsen.com/content/dam/corporate/us/en/reports-downloads/2016-reports/nielsen-asian-american-consumer-report-may-2016.pdf.

Okazaki, Sumie. "Influences of Culture on Asian-Americans' Sexuality." *Journal of Sex Research* 39, no. 1 (2002) 34–41.

Palmer, Parker. *Let Your Life Speak: Listening for the Voice of Vocation.* San Francisco: Jossey-Bass, 2000.

Pariser, Eli. *The Filter Bubble: What the Internet Is Hiding from You.* New York: Penguin, 2011.

Park, Andrew Sung. *The Wounded Heart of God: The Asian Concept of Han and the Christian Doctrine of Sin.* Nashville: Abingdon, 1993.

Petersen, William. "Success Story, Japanese-American Style." *The New York Times Magazine,* January 6, 1966, 20–43.

Peterson, Eugene H. *The Message: The Bible in Contemporary Language.* Colorado Springs, CO: NavPress, 2002.

Pew Research Center. "The Rise of Asian Americans." April 4, 2013 (updated edition). http://www.pewsocialtrends.org/2012/06/19/the-rise-of-asian-americans/.

Phan, Peter C. "Betwixt and Between: Doing Theology with Memory and Imagination." In *Toward an Autobiographical Theology in American-Asian Perspective*, edited by Peter Phan and Jung Young Lee, 113–33. Collegeville, MN: Liturgical, 1999.

———. *Christianity With an Asian Face: Asian American Theology in the Making.* Maryknoll, NY: Orbis, 2003.

Phinney, Jean. "Ethnic Identity and Acculturation." In *Acculturation: Advances in Theory, Measurement, and Applied Research*, edited by Kevin Chun et al., 63–81. American Psychological Association, 2003.

Piper, John. *Desiring God: Meditations of a Christian Hedonist.* Sisters, OR: Multnomah, 1996.

Prasso, Sheridan. *The Asian Mystique: Dragon Ladies, Geisha Girls, & Our Fantasies of the Exotic Orient.* New York: PublicAffairs, 2005.

Rah, Soong-Chan. *The Next Evangelicalism: Freeing the Church from Western Cultural Captivity.* Downers Grove, IL: InterVarsity Press, 2009.

Redman, Beth, and Matt Redman. "Blessed Be Your Name." *Where Angels Fear to Tread.* Survivor, 2002.

Rizzuto, Ana-Maria. *The Birth of the Living God: A Psychological Study.* Chicago: University of Chicago Press, 1979.

Roland, Alan. *Cultural Pluralism and Psychoanalysis: The Asian and North American Experience.* New York: Routledge, 1996.

Scott, James C. *Domination and the Arts of Resistance: Hidden Transcripts.* New Haven, CT: Yale University Press, 1990.

———. *Weapons of the Weak: Everyday Forms of Peasant Resistance.* New Haven, CT: Yale University Press, 1987.

Selznick, Philip. *The Moral Commonwealth: Social Theory and the Promise of Community.* Berkeley, CA: University of California Press, 1992.

Setran, David P., and Chris A. Kiesling. *Spiritual Formation of Emerging Adulthood: A Practical Theology for College and Young Adult Ministry.* Grand Rapids: Baker Academic, 2013.

Sherman, Amy L. *Kingdom Calling: Vocational Stewardship for the Common Good.* Downers Grove, IL: InterVarsity Press, 2011.

Shyong, Frank. "Sriracha Hot Sauce Purveyor Turns up the Heat." *Los Angeles Times*, April 12, 2013.

———. "Sriracha Sauce Becomes a Hot Political Issue with Bipartisan Backing." In *Los Angeles Times*, May 2, 2014.

Siegel, Daniel J. *The Developing Mind, Second Edition: How Relationships and the Brain Interact to Shape Who We Are.* 2nd ed. New York: Guilford, 2015.

Smedes, Lewis B. *Sex for Christians: The Limits and Liberties of Sexual Living.* Grand Rapids: Eerdmans, 1994.

Stark, Rodney. *The Rise of Christianity.* Princeton, NJ: Princeton University Press, 1996.

Stassen, Glen H., and David P. Gushee. *Kingdom Ethics: Following Jesus in Contemporary Context.* Downers Grove, IL: InterVarsity Press, 2003.

Stuart, Elizabeth. "The Theological Study of Sexuality." In *The Oxford Handbook of Theology, Sexuality, and Gender*, edited by Adrian Thatcher, 18–31. Oxford: Oxford University Press, 2015.

Sue, Derald Wing, and David Sue. *Counseling the Culturally Diverse: Theory and Practice.* 6th ed. New York: Wiley, 2013.

Sue, Stanley, and James K. Morishima. *The Mental Health of Asian Americans.* San Francisco: Josey-Bass, 1982.

Tang, Mei. "A Comparison of Asian American, Caucasian American, and Chinese College Students: An Initial Report." *Journal of Multicultural Counseling and Development* 30 (2002) 124–34.

Tanner, Kathryn. *Theories of Culture: A New Agenda for Theology.* Minneapolis: Fortress, 1997.

Tatum, Beverly. *Why Are All the Black Kids Sitting Together in the Cafeteria? And Other Conversations about Race.* New York: Basic, 2003.

Thomsen, Jacqueline. "The Asian American Achievement Paradox." *Inside Higher Ed,* August 4, 2015. https://www.insidehighered.com/news/2015/08/04/authors-discuss-reasoning-behind-high-levels-asian-american-achievement.

Tong, Vuying. "Acculturation, Gender Disparity, and the Sexual Behavior of Asian American Youth." *Journal of Sex Research* 50, no. 6 (2013) 560–73.

Toyama, Nikki A. "Getting Used to the Sound of My Voice." In *Asian American Christian Reader,* edited by Viji Nakka-Cammauf and Timothy Tseng, 167–76. Castro Valley, CA: Pacific Asian American Canadian Christian Educational Project & The Institute for the Study of Asian American Christianity, 2009.

Tuan, Mia. *Forever Foreigners or Honorary Whites? The Asian Ethnic Experience Today.* New Brunswick, NJ: Rutgers University Press, 1999.

Turkle, Sherry. *Alone Together: Why We Expect More from Technology and Less from Each Other.* New York: Basic, 2011.

Turpin, Katherine. "Adolescence: Vocation in Performance, Passion, and Possibility." In *Calling All Years Good: Christian Vocation throughout Life's Seasons,* edited by Kathleen A. Cahalan and Bonnie J. Miller-McLemore, 76–91. Grand Rapids: Eerdmans, 2017.

———. "Younger Adulthood." In *Calling All Years Good: Christian Vocation throughout Life's Seasons,* edited by Kathleen A. Cahalan and Bonnie J. Miller-McLemore, 95–122. Grand Rapids; Eerdmans, 2017.

Volf, Miroslav. *Exclusion and Embrace: A Theological Exploration of Identity, Otherness, and Reconciliation.* Nashville: Abingdon, 1996.

Wallis, Jim. *The (Un)Common Good: How the Gospel Brings Hope to a World Divided.* Grand Rapids: Brazos, 2014.

Wan, Sze-Kar. "Asian American Perspectives: Ambivalence of the Model Minority and Perpetual Foreigner." In *Studying Paul's Letters: Contemporary Perspectives and Methods,* edited by Joseph A. Marchal, 175–90. Minneapolis: Fortress, 2012.

Wang, Philip. "What Asian Parents Don't Say . . . " YouTube video. December 24, 2015. https://youtu.be/Myou629Dk68.

Weiler, Jeanne Drysdale. *Codes and Contradictions: Race, Gender Identity, and Schooling Power, Social Identity, and Education.* New York: State University of New York Press, 2000.

Wenham, Gordon J. *Genesis.* Word Biblical Commentary. Waco, TX: Word, 1987.

Wilhelm, Richard. *Confucius and Confucianism.* Arkana: Penguin, 1967.

Williams, Patricia. *The Alchemy of Race and Rights: Diary of a Law Professor.* Cambridge, MA: Harvard University Press, 1991.

Wimmer, A., and K. Lewis. "Beyond and Below Racial Homophily: Erg Models of a Friendship Network Documented on Facebook." *American Journal of Sociology* 116, no. 2 (2010) 583–642.

Winner, Lauren F. *Real Sex: The Naked Truth About Chastity.* Grand Rapids: Brazos, 2006.

Wong Fu Productions. "What Asian Parents Don't Say . . ." YouTube video, 3:57. https://youtube/Myoout629Dk68.

Wu, Ellen D. *The Color of Success: Asian Americans and the Origins of the Model Minority.* Princeton, NJ: Princeton University Press, 2015.

Wu, Frank H. "How Do Asian Americans Advocate for Equality without Throwing Other People of Color Under the Bus?" *The Huffington Post,* April 9, 2016 (updated April 10, 2017). http://www.huffingtonpost.com/frank-h-wu/how-do-asian-americans-ad_b_9650828.html.

————. *Yellow: Race in America Beyond Black and White.* Reprint ed. New York: Basic, 2003.

Wu, Jean Yu-wen Shen, and Thomas C. Chen, eds. *Asian Americans Studies Now: A Critical Reader.* New Brunswick, NJ: Rutgers University Press, 2012.

Yang, Wesley. "Paper Tigers: What Happens to All the Asian-American Overachievers When the Test-Taking Ends?" *New York Magazine,* May 8, 2011. http://nymag.com/news/features/asian-americans-2011-5/

Yao, Xinzhong. *An Introduction to Confucianism.* Cambridge: Cambridge University Press, 2000.

Yee, Gale A. "'She Stood in Tears Amid the Alien Corn': Ruth, the Perpetual Foreigner and the Model Minority." In *They Were All Together in One Place? Toward Minority Biblical Criticism,* edited by Randall C. Bailey, et al., 119–40. Atlanta: Society of Biblical Literature, 2009.

Yu, Henry. *Thinking Orientals: Migration, Contact, and Exoticism in Modern America.* New York: Oxford University Press, 2001.

INDEX

Index

Made in the USA
Monee, IL
13 November 2019